Women and Madness

Feminist Perspectives

Series Editor: Michelle Stanworth

Published

Seyla Benhabib and Drucilla Cornell (eds.), *Feminism as Critique*
Harriet Bradley, *Men's Work, Women's Work*
Felicia Gordon, *The Integral Feminist: Madeleine Pelletier, 1874–1939*
Susanne Kappeler, *The Pornography of Representation*
Liz Kelly, *Surviving Sexual Violence*
Judy Lown, *Women and Industrialization*
Henrietta L. Moore, *Feminism and Anthropology*
June Purvis, *Hard Lessons: The Lives and Education of Working-Class
    Women in Nineteenth-Century England*
Yannick Ripa, *Women and Madness*
Barbara Sichtermann, *Femininity: The Politics of the Personal*
Michelle Stanworth (ed.), *Reproductive Technologies*
Sylvia Walby, *Patriarchy at Work*

WOMEN AND MADNESS

The Incarceration of Women in Nineteenth-Century France

YANNICK RIPA

Translated by Catherine du Peloux Menagé

University of Minnesota Press

This English translation copyright © 1990 by Polity Press

First published as *La ronde des folles*. © Aubier, 1986, Paris

Published by the University of Minnesota Press
2037 University Avenue Southeast, Minneapolis, MN 55414
Printed in Great Britain

ISBN 0–8166–1929–8

Library of Congress Cataloging-in-Publication Data

A CIP catalogue record for this book is available from the Library of Congress.

LC number: 90–050447

TP

CONTENTS

For Jeannette and César

INTRODUCTION

'One, two three, women are all crazy, except for my nanny who makes apple pie . . .' This sixteenth-century nursery rhyme, which children in the Ile de France were still singing three hundred years later, seemed cruelly true in nineteenth-century France. Between 1845 and 1849 there were 9,930 madwomen concealed behind the walls of asylums, and this had risen to 19,692 in 1871. This frightening increase suggested that all women are potential lunatics; that the eternal feminine walks a tightrope and goes through life depending on a thread which might break at any moment and plunge womankind into the abyss of madness. Moreover, it was believed that the inherent physical weakness of women and their obvious mental fragility were very closely linked. Women's bodies were taken over by their devouring wombs which destroyed their mental health. Under attack from emotions, imagination and all sorts of passions, the female body writhed, its tendons shook, limbs cracked, and blood was carried to the head. This is the picture of female insanity: bare-breasted women, their sexual organs exposed to public view, creatures incapable of thought, staring out blankly. Admittedly, this was the result of mental disturbance, but these women were also out of control. Madness was the fruit of their diseased senses; madness was physical as well as mental.

This is the vision of female madness constructed by the iconography of the period. Literature also played its part. On rereading even the most classic of nineteenth-century works, we are forced to an unexpected conclusion. It was impossible to write without touching on the subject of female madness; it was everywhere. In Balzac's works, for example, madness affects twenty-six women. The lives of his characters reflect the gradual increase of madness, which was built on women's notorious 'fragile nerves'. Any excessive expression of emotion was seen as the forerunner of a frenzied attack. Neurosis took on many shapes – spleen and melancholia, moving on to 'hysteria' and then straight madness. Insanity cut off the madwoman from the rest of the world – be it the congenital madness of Geneviève the imbecile, or the accidental madness of Stéphanie, the two heroines of Balzac's *L'Adieu*.

Madness was a constant dialectical element in the lives of Zola's heroes. To take away madness from Zola's work is to take away its very essence. It is the sap which feeds the tree of the Rougon-Macquart, it is diluted in the blood of the descendants of Aunt Dide, the mad old woman locked up in the asylum of the Tulettes. The entire life of the family was articulated around lunacy, which reappears in many guises. Insanity was hiding behind Gervaise's alcoholism in *L'Assommoir*, was confirmed by the hysteria and vice of Anna Coupeau, the heroine of *Nana*, and was blatantly clear in the imbecility of Désirée (*La Faute de l'abbé Mouret*).

Beyond the concerns of individual writers, the main driving force behind their pen was their concern for 'reality and truth'.[1] Take for example the Goncourt brothers. The fictionalized story of the betrayal of their maid Rose Malingre became a detailed description of the hysteria of Germinie Lacerteux.

Mental illness was also present in popular literature. Serializations in newspapers portrayed a different image of madness. Whereas in bourgeois literature, madness, latent or manifest, was an intrinsic part of the person concerned, in the lives of the heroines of pulp literature, it was only an accident. Descriptions of insanity did not aim at exploring the depths of the character's soul. Instead, these descriptions sought to make the reader weep or applaud. Madness was part of the range of misfortunes visited upon the innocent heroine. It was also one of the punishments inflicted on the wicked – La Frochard in *Deux orphelines*. In the first case madness was the last straw, the epitome of injustice, and in the second it was a punishment better than death, which would be too much. It was a half-death, the death of the mind.

Endless further examples could be found. They would only confirm the psychological fascination of madness in the minds of the people of that period. Their imagination was both fuelled by very real statistics, and comforted by seeing those feudal edifices, the asylums. But to the man in the street, things were simple. More asylums meant more madness. The ordinary person understood little more than this. Women in particular seemed to be affected by a dramatic increase in the incidence of madness, but in reality the levels of insanity in both sexes were affected.

Asylums were officially born in 1838. A new law dealing with insanity, termed 'loi de police et de bienfaisance' decreed that in every *département* a public institution should be set up with the specific aim of taking in and treating the insane. Two types of committal were established. Voluntary committal was a private matter, requested by a third party, most commonly by a parent, with the backing of a doctor from outside the asylum. Official committal was a matter for the prefect to decide, again with external medical opinion. Asylums were thus set up to look after the insane, but their main real aim was to protect society. These 'special hospitals', as they were called, were a place for observing and silencing any behaviour which could be seen as threatening to the family or to society. This new 'alienist' medicine flirted with religion, morality and the police; in a sense, it became the keeper of public order.

Yet public order was not satisfied with vague definitions; the authorities relied on accurate labelling of deviant individuals. A precise system of classifying illness was necessary, rather than a broad characterization of madness as the opposite of sanity. Descriptions of the various types of insanity were supposed to be totally objective. The masters of this enterprise were the 'alienist doctors' or 'alienists'. From this point on, they were the only people acknowledged as qualified to identify madness.

Insanity had become a matter for medical diagnosis; the insane were no longer merely lunatics. They now had a status; to be sure, they were only patients, but at least now they existed. This new situation gave even more power to these so-called special doctors. Their knowledge of the workings of the mind gave them a mysterious or even a magical aura in the eyes of ordinary people. The charisma of their position meant that they were simultaneously feared, admired and respected. These psychiatrists were the bearers of a new type of knowledge which they proclaimed loudly, and their words were greeted with the deference 'which is granted to scientific assertions which are too young to have been challenged'.[2] The power of these few men of science also made them a driving force in preventive medicine, then in its infancy. Since they were qualified to intervene in moments of crisis, they were also qualified to point out how to live in order to avoid these crises.

The world of the alienist was the world of the bourgeoisie and alienists were a vehicle for bourgeois ideology. They adopted a typically bourgeois method of spreading this ideology: philanthropy. This explains the constant references to Pinel who was elevated to the rank of spiritual ancestor. The image of the 'liberator of the mad' stood at the junction of philosophy and medicine. He was credited with having established the idea that madness could be treated. This basic assumption was necessary if the lunatic was to enter the medical system. From then on, the clinical eye was able to identify the types of behaviour which led to madness.

This meant that madness could now be tracked down and definitions of insanity became increasingly broad in order to narrow down the parameters of 'normal' behaviour. Only such normal behaviour was sanctioned. The 'great confinement' was accompanied by intensive labelling of people. General and psychiatric doctors, not to mention specialists who quibbled over definitions, may have diverged diagnostically but they were all agreed on one point: the people identified by their system were definitely mad and had to be removed from society to be cared for within institutions set up for that specific purpose. These were the asylums.

From 1838 onwards asylums reigned in France. The entire country was convinced that it had found the answer to the problem of the existence of lunatics. The creators of the special hospitals thought that they had invented the only environment suitable for the treatment of madness. Asylums were societies separate from the lives of normal people; they had their own rhythms, rules, laws, and their own particular social and economic structures. To define these unique places, a new vocabulary was created, though it seems anachronistic to us now. Words like *placement* (committal), *maintenance* (to keep in an asylum), *transfert, translation* (transfer), *asile* (asylum), *asilation, asilement* (being placed in an asylum): these and other neologisms were invented to describe the new situation.

The new institutions were seen to have some shortcomings, but the psychiatrists (or alienists, to give them their nineteenth-century name) blamed this on the fact that the idea was so new. Gradually, this excuse lost any value it might have had. Towards 1860 severe criticisms were levelled at the material inadequacies of the institutions for the insane. Even the law governing the treatment of the insane was called into question. But in 1838 the most important thing was that the medical profession had found an institution which made it possible for doctors to put their theories into practice. It is in this context that the present account will examine the ways in which asylums functioned. My aim is not to retell the story of the special hospitals, but to examine the background to the 'moral treatment' undertaken in asylums, and the minor changes which occurred during the period we will be looking at.

It is no coincidence that the peak of the importance of asylums (from 1830 to 1860) was a period which had a symptom-based approach to disease. This involved rejecting all organic causes and only believing in moral causes. From 1790 to 1800 onwards, psychiatry took on a moralizing tone. It was believed that therapy should be aimed at the healthy part of the person in order to struggle against the sick part; the doctor's own qualities would supplement the patient's deficiencies; one mind would help another. This was the fundamental change of the early part of the century, and not the fact that lunatics were freed from their chains in 1793.

But despite the fact that this was the era of positivism, the subjective nature of the therapeutic process is striking. Because there could be no answer to the eternal question 'what is madness?', the consequences of this approach were much worse. The labels attached to diseases could be problematic, and varied depending on time and place. It became difficult to distinguish between the symptoms, the disease itself and the different forms it took. In spite of all assertions to the contrary, mental illness remained a special sort of disease. It was still characterized in terms of its opposite, and still led to the patient being rejected by society.

It is this very difficulty in defining madness which makes it possible for us today to attempt different readings of the available information. Was the golden age of 'alienism' somehow conducive to mental imbalance, or was the rapid expansion in the population of asylums the result of the nature of madness itself? Were women really weaker, more prone to madness, as the received wisdom of that time would have it, an idea which is still alive today?

This book seeks to answer these questions. There are medical records to help in our investigations, but unfortunately the law on hospital archives makes it impossible to consult registers dating from later than 1850; however, publications of the time do not suggest that any great changes took place in the following decade.

We should always remember that there are two ways of looking at madness; it can be observed from the outside or experienced from the inside. The difference between experience and observation is always passed over in silence and the hidden story of madness is never told. The pages which follow try to listen to that silence and to hear the stifled cries within it.

Part I

SLIPPING INTO MADNESS

1

Outcasts from Society

The hospital covered thirty-one hectares. Its paths were as long as roads. It contained innumerable buildings organized into districts, exercise yards, isolated chalets, and even a tavern which doubled as a café and a shop for the basic requirements of life. It was a city of four thousand inhabitants within the City; and what a city! It teemed with people who wandered about, crying, wailing, piled into cramped dormitories. The Salpêtrière of the 1840s was indeed a city, a capital city, the capital of female suffering, poverty and insanity. Behind high walls it was like a quarantine station for Paris, and housed women suffering from physical diseases, elderly paupers as well as madwomen. This Parisian monument to female confinement stood out because it was not only a 'special hospital' but also a general hospital and a home for the elderly. But the burden of the 800 to 1,400 madwomen it housed from 1836 to 1860 was to overshadow the hospital's other roles.

The Salpêtrière had previously been a hospital for vice. It had housed syphilitic prostitutes, who were partly prisoners and partly patients and who often spent the last years of their lives senile and insane. The hospital never lived down its past history, not helped by the fact that it continued to house prostitutes. In the popular mind the Salpêtrière meant vice and madness. These two labels carried a stigma which remained attached to all its inhabitants. Even when they were cured the patients would never again be like other women. In that way they were like prisoners, who after serving their sentence would become ex-convicts. And leaving the Salpêtrière was very like being released from prison! The vocabulary used to describe it fed this ambiguity. After having been 'sequestered, confined, deprived of freedom, isolated' (sometimes in cells using methods of coercion which might include chains), if the madwoman hadn't escaped, she was 'freed, returned to society, given back her freedom'. These expressions show that the pretensions of asylums masked their true function as places where lunatics were kept safe behind walls. This reminds us, should that be necessary, that committal was more often than not a matter for the police. 'More often than not' changed to 'always' as official committals increased disproportionately from 1844 onwards; they became dominant and in 1853 accounted for 80 per cent of committals.

From the streets to the cells

The patients of the Salpêtrière all followed a similar path to the asylum. The only differences were different starting points. They had often sought refuge in churches or the entrance halls of apartment blocks. For example, Josephine, a young prisoner freed after nineteen months in prison, was discovered by a concierge huddled in a stairwell, trembling with fear. She was arrested and charged with vagrancy; her incoherence led her to the Salpêtrière. There she met Marthe whose obsession with prayer and swaying walk had attracted the attention of her parish priest. Every day she would wait for the archangel who was, she said, going to give her a mission. The priest notified the authorities of the 'Bureau Central'.

Set up in 1796, taking over from the police commission, this body consisted of eight specialized divisions with specific responsibilities: intelligence, public safety, public morality and public opinion, prisons, health and hygiene, internal waterways, homes for the elderly and wet nurses. A detailed report was prepared every month for the Minister of the Interior. The Bureau Central, like the newly-created 'Assistance Publique' made it possible to track down deviants, to keep tight control over fringe milieux in liaison with the police. Improvements in its structure at the time made it particularly effective. It was directly involved in most official committals.

The police would arrest the most glaring pathological cases in the streets. For example, Adèle was waving her arms, trying to fly – she wanted to get back to her nest hidden under the rooftops; Marie sat in the middle of the road preaching to invisible cats. Clémence assaulted passers-by whom she saw as the devil in disguise. The little birds and the high priestesses would often be led handcuffed to the police headquarters, that meeting place of the mad from the streets, as criminals indicted by their own

ravings. Then a long pathetic wait would begin. The cells of Paris
were far from having the necessary sanitary facilities. The former
asylum inmate Hersilie Rouy, whose story will be told later,
remembered in her memoirs her stay in this disgusting place
where the walls were covered in excrement. It was a small cell
closed by two large locks on the outside, the only light came from
a barred skylight. Underneath it there was 'an enormous pipe
without a lid for personal needs. The furniture consisted of two
straw mattresses as filthy as the walls and on them were rolled up
two grey woollen blankets.[1]

This picture was made worse by overcrowding and lack of
privacy. No medical services were provided and patients were
not grouped according to different types of illnesses. Hersilie was
joined by a peaceful madwoman from Charenton, an epileptic
and two idiots. 'Once we were all in, they brought us each a bowl
of soup, with enough fat on the top to float a wick on and use as a
lamp, a big piece of meat and an even bigger piece of bread –
basically enough so that we didn't die of hunger, and all of it in
wooden bowls with spoons of the same.'[2]

These disgraceful conditions were denounced in vain by health
inspectors. Sadly they were by no means exclusive to Paris. A
report to the prefect of the Dordogne complained about the fact
that lunatics had a long wait without any treatment in conditions
similar to those described above, before being admitted to
Leymes. Transport was only arranged when there was a sufficiently
large number of lunatics to make it 'profitable'![3] In Paris
administrative delays often meant stays in the cells for several
days. Though they didn't know it, the patients were waiting for
the prefect's decree, issued on a special form, which would state
that person X 'is in a state of insanity which may jeopardize
public order and public safety', in the words of the initial indictment. The patient had to be certified insane by two doctors. The
prefect would then nominate a special hospital, where the committed patient was to be 'treated for the illness with which s/he is
afflicted, which has shown itself in wild behaviour'. These ready-
made phrases show how rigidly the law of 1836 was being applied.
Since it was passed, it had oscillated between two poles – charity
and policing. The figures we have seem to say that the time for
hesitation was over. Only protection and profitability counted.
The law protected society by taking care of lunatics.

'Dangerousness'

The law did not look on madness as an illness to be treated.
Rather, it saw it as a danger to be contained and neutralized.
Letters from the prefects endlessly insisted on the violence which
was felt to lie dormant in every patient. The feature which the
authorities called 'dangerousness' became the motivation for the
policy of assistance to the insane. The Dechambre dictionary
specifies that 'this state of danger must represent something
current and positive, that is, an imminent danger for the mad
person or for society from the point of view of safety, order and
morality.'[4] It was not therefore a psychiatric concept. Because it
was so undefinable, boundless and variable, 'dangerousness' was
a wonderful instrument in the hands of the authorities. Of course,
the concept changed depending on the political party in power,
and with the types of behaviour that that party was prepared to
sanction in accordance with its model of power.

The inordinate increase in official committals was not due to an
epidemic of madness undermining Paris. The capital was experi-
encing the calm period of the first part of the century; the
administrative area, the department of the Seine, dominated by
Paris, came only twenty-sixth in the statistics of criminal activity
by department. No, the astronomical rise in the population of
asylums was a measure, not of the level of insanity, but of the fear
of the owning and ruling classes. They were terrified of madness,
which was for them a dormant, subterranean power, a volcano on
which Paris was dancing. Madness was seen as a biological
component in the make-up of the working class, an intrinsic
element of their psychology. The increase in the population of
Paris, due to the general increase in the population of France and
to the predominantly male exodus from the countryside, reinforced
their fears. The bourgeois mind was haunted by the image of
Paris as a town afflicted by the diseases of poverty, madness and
violence.

The law of 1838 was the death knell to all hopes of the
possibility of integrating the insane into society; it was the end of
the image passed down from antiquity of the madman as bearer
of truths, the end of the idea of 'the village idiot'. The collapse of
community life led to the exclusion of the insane, since they were
not integrated and could not be integrated into the new
developing society. Those who were potentially mentally ill
slipped through the wide mesh of the urban net, and only

emerged later, after their madness had exploded, after they had committed an act which marked them out as insane. By then, it was much too late. The powers that be, the defenders of public peace, the protectors of bourgeois society had to intervene before the inevitable happened. Because the authorities narrowed down the limits of permissible behaviour, and increasingly associated madness and danger, they set in motion the huge increase in official committals which we have already described.

The reasons given for official committal to asylums certainly give us an insight into mental illness, but they also shed light on the unconscious mind of the authorities, dissecting their hidden anguish and unveiling their hidden fantasies. This is the angle from which official committal must be studied. From this point of view only borderline cases deserve our attention, since they are the only ones which show the boundaries between normality and madness. Cases where the illness is self-evident will only appear as statistics in this book: we will not, for example, study the case of a monomaniac admitted because he thought he was a dog! However, it is important to be aware that the choice of this restricted definition reflects this writer's personal attitude to madness, contemporary attitudes and the limitations which we today set on our conception of madness.

Keeping the streets safe

Order, security and vagrancy are antitheses. In the midst of all sorts of drop-outs and fringe dwellers who set up home in the streets, the police discovered women reduced to vagrancy because they could not survive living alone. The same reason was given for committing female idiots, imbeciles, and, strangely enough, old people. The association of these different groups tells us that the concepts of disease of the period were more social than medical.

The proportion of idiots, imbeciles and cretins (see glossary) was so high that from 1845 alienists had to distinguish between them and the insane. Initially, asylums had swallowed up all the feeble-minded, even in rural areas. But the reception facilities of the hospitals constrained the authorities to push back the tide. As early as 1842 a letter from the prefect of the lower Loire[5] ordered that the feeble-minded be kept in their home areas, and opposed the official committal of these people. As for voluntary committal, used by families more and more, following the example set from

above, it was authorized by the authorities of the prefecture only
if the inmate was paid for.

Free medical care was therefore restricted; in some departments,
even among those officially committed it was reserved for
paupers suffering from a major form of madness. Implemented
across the whole of France, these measures bore fruit. In 1866, 90
per cent of idiots remained in their families while the majority of
the insane (63 per cent) were behind walls. Paris had a particular
problem; the feeble-minded lost themselves in the anonymity of
the big city; given their poor memory and general incoherence,
they were unable to reconstruct their past. Unable to take them
back to their homes, the police gave them different homes:
asylums.

The provinces were aware of the opportunity this gave them to
get rid of undesirable cases. Aglaé, Justine, Augustine and very
many others arrived in Paris by train, a journey on which they
would certainly not have been able to start without help! Since
they were potentially dangerous, they ended up increasing the
already overpopulated Salpêtrière.

The other marginal figures of Parisian society were old people.
They belonged to the same subworld of deprivation and sank into
poverty and its attendant ills, becoming vagrants and beggars.
Eugenie fought with pigeons for the crumbs of bread thrown by a
passer-by. Anne-Claude held out her hand to beg, totally unable
to say a word. Since there was no organized welfare system,
destitution became a psychiatric symptom. The fact that women
lived slightly longer, and particularly their poorly paid positions,
made them more likely to become victims of this situation than
men. The authorities of the prefecture and the doctors responsible
for committals backed up the action of the police.

Confusing old age and insanity in this way was often
denounced by alienists. After the initial period of observation
only senile madwomen and those of feeble minds were kept in
the asylums. Those whom the doctors called 'old and poor rather
than insane' were directed towards other appropriate institutions.
The expression 'sent to the paupers' section' recurs constantly in
the files of the Salpêtrière. But the efforts of the special doctors
were not enough to eliminate entirely this dumping of elderly
people who had regressed to childhood. The medical inspectors
Constans, Lunier, Dumesnil emphasized this tendency and noted
the sad fact that there were more women than men involved; they
counted 167 old women who were not mad as against 109 men in
ten asylums which they visited in 1874.[6]

The slightest threat to public order was seen as a danger which had to be contained. This, together with the inability to live alone, was the most frequent motive for the official committal of women. Speaking aggressively and shouting insults out loud could count as psychiatric symptoms. Women tended to express aggression through speech rather than actions. Blows, wounds and homicides belonged to the world of male violence. This gender-based difference in behaviour could have been because female patients had partly internalized the current social model of the sweet and submissive woman. But it could also be explained by the suppression of any sign of behaviour which might transgress beyond the strict boundaries of permitted behaviour. For example, Madeleine's flowery language and loud tones disturbed the peace of the apartment block where she was the concierge, and the police had her committed to the Salpêtrière. The law didn't hesitate to intervene even within the family, and even to act for parents who did not dare take the step which would lead to the special hospital. In 1866, Françoise, who was 'creating a disturbance at the home of a member of her family' was arrested and sent to the Salpêtrière.

The Paris police carried out the orders from the authorities to the letter. A letter from the prefect of police dated 16 April 1846 insisted on the need to keep order within Paris. Faced with a large population

> mostly made up of people who are strangers to each other . . . it was necessary to be sure in the general interest to take prompt measures which, in a smaller town, could have been put off without creating problems. A patient whom it would be easier to supervise in a place where everyone knew him . . . becomes dangerous in Paris where he . . . would be bound to escape if special measures were not applied and the person were not committed to the special care of a hospice.[7]

As a result of this, women who refused to conform and genuine cases of madness could be mixed up, and rebellion could become a symptom of mental illness. This was the story of Miss L told by Hersilie Rouy. An illegitimate child, Miss L was given to the care of her grandfather. Her mother took her away hoping to get money for the child from the grandparent. Her blackmail tactics failed and L stayed with her mother who had a very unorthodox lifestyle. The men around her took her to brothels, where she met army officers who took her to Algeria. On returning to Paris, Miss L learned of the deaths of her grandfather and her father. The latter had acknowledged her legally just before his death, so she tried to recover some of her inheritance. But, probably having been given the wrong information, she went to the police. Without knowing it she had made the first step towards being crushed in a deadly machine.

As a loose woman only her body seemed to count, her words had no weight. The head clerk in the prefecture 'tried to kiss her' instead of listening to her request. Miss L fought him off and thrashed him; because she refused to give in, she had to be diminished; the policeman who felt his manhood under threat, ridiculed by a prostitute, had Miss L committed to the Salpêtrière. Then her anger exploded against the medical staff; the doctors immediately ordered that she should be transferred to Orléans, an easy way of getting rid of a troublemaker who refused to give in to the rule of psychiatry. But she continued to cause trouble and because of her stubbornness she was admitted to the Sanitas, the section for manic patients.

The case of Miss L, which was in no way unusual, illustrates both the ways in which the law of 1838 could be misused for repressive purposes and the way in which female deviant behaviour could become a psychiatric issue. Being aggressive to the police would lead men to prison and women to the asylum. These different destinations are revealing: male agression against the police force was punished for being an assault on the established order, and therefore was a matter for the justice system; but Miss L's aggressiveness towards the police was not seen as a matter for punishment but for treatment. Women who expressed their aggression were mad. It was not that they dared to express this aggression which was seen as an act of madness but *having* aggressive and violent feelings at all; those were male characteristics. In expressing feelings of this kind a woman was making her abnormality so clear that she obviously deserved to be sent to the Sanitas.

The harshness of this measure didn't surprise Hersilie Rouy. Although she never stopped fighting against imprisonment in asylums, she felt no solidarity with Miss L. By her birth, her life and her violent behaviour, Miss L was totally at odds with society. A defender of bourgeois Christian morality, Hersilie rejected her and without knowing it spoke for the public opinion of her time. Today Miss L's sad past would be seen as a prime factor in creating a major neurosis; doctors would talk of the trauma of illegitimacy experienced as shameful, they would invoke her emotional break with the paternal milieu which she doubtless idealized, the way in which she was used as merchandise between her two parents, the fact that she grew up on the fringes of society in an immoral milieu where the female body and female beauty made women into mercenary objects in the hands of men . . . and so on.

But for Hersilie Rouy there were no extenuating circumstances. Miss L's past wasn't the cause of madness, it *was* madness. Illegitimate birth was seen as a cause of degeneration, her great beauty and her family background inevitably led to prostitution – the bourgeois nineteenth century liked moderation in all things. In Hersilie's mind, prostitution and madness were symbiotic. The admission of Miss L, as of all loose women, was therefore quite justified.

Prostitution is not only the oldest profession, it is also, according to some doctors of the time, a defect which has a physiological cause. This theory of how women are born prostitutes was championed by the Italian psychiatrist Lombroso, the founder of criminal anthropology. He believed that the physical constitution of prostitutes differentiated them from good women: they were said to have a small brain and eye capacity, astonishingly heavy mandibles, the occipital bone was said to be hypertrophied and irregular, their foreheads wide and their nasal bones abnormal. Other stigmata of prostitutes were an asymmetrical face and eyebrows. The whore-by-birth could also apparently be recognized because she had fat thighs, she was small and unusually hairy. These excesses and the size of the vocal cords linked prostitution to masculinity. The analogy was not particularly new but Lombroso's originality was that his politico-philosophical discourse was veiled in scientific language.[8]

However, the police were not up to applying these anthropomorphic criteria. Public safety was too important for these nuances. Leading a debauched lifestyle, loose morals and vice were the reasons given for committing Thérèse and Antoinette, Géraldine and Camille. These so-called 'reasons' were really accusations. Thérèse, a fifty-three-year-old seamstress, was committed in 1843 because her debauched lifestyle was said to be harmful to public order; in her medical files Doctor Baillarger put forward her 'unorthodox previous life and her habit of going to public places of entertainment, shows, dances, etc. This dissipated life nevertheless did not show the disorderly behaviour which so often went hand in hand with sexual excesses.' Thérèse, who was committed officially, demanded 'to be freed, often, with no attempt at justification', as the special doctor specified, 'mainly so that she could go back to the Grande Chaumière and go out with carabiniers to Varsailles'.[9] She was clearly unaware that she was repeating the same eccentricities that had been seen originally as signs of madness.

As for Antoinette-Jeanne, she was admitted because of her seductive behaviour, seen as an expression of madness. The medical records of the Salpêtrière of 1841 specified that: 'Her dissolute life was such that her manic fits would often become part of the disordered and corrupt scenes over which she presided. One of her methods of seduction was to pass herself off as the widow of General Bonnaire, unhappy and illustrious victim of the reactionary outburst of 1815.'[10]

It was only a step from prostitution to erotomania. Erotomania was queen in the kingdom of deviances which resulted in official committal. But like prostitution (which could be obvious, suspected, seductive) the term covered different types of behaviour. Geraldine is admitted because her behaviour was 'extremely lewd'. 'When her husband wants to see her, she reproaches him with failing to do his duty; he shouldn't be coming to the visiting room but to the bedroom. She reveals her sexual organs to men and inserts a large stone into her vagina.'[11]

What did this behaviour have in common with Camille? Camille's mental imbalance showed itself in her 'flaunting herself' with a man twenty years her junior, in her shop – a public place. The affection which she showed towards him in the sight of all led her to the Salpêtrière as an erotomane.[12]

The male reaction to the fluidity of female behaviour was rigid. Dissolute behaviour had to be condemned; venal or seductive female sexuality had to be silenced. It was necessary to commit erotomanes suffering from lubricious mania, uterine fury, hysterical mania, erotic mania, tendency towards masturbation, or nymphomania because this unbridled sexual activity went against the plan for a socially controlled sexuality, where desire and pleasure were male prerogatives. Committing prostitutes was the result of the phobia of syphilis of those in power and of their fears of psychological degeneration which might contaminate the whole of society. Committal was therefore fighting against the global danger represented by the concentration of the lower classes in the capital. In the provinces where there were fewer whores, who were therefore easier to control, there was more tolerance. There, prostitution was seen as a 'necessary evil' answering sexual needs.

Criminology: an outline

As we have seen, in Paris the special hospital was indubitably one of the main cogs in a coercive machine set up to fight prostitution. Between prisons and asylums there came to exist a very disturbing system of communication, regulated partly by medical expertise. This led to the creation of a new medical cum legal method of criminal analysis. Judges by no means always resorted to this method, and thus they slowed down the will to power of the alienists and protected themselves from attempts to encroach on their own territory. Crimes had to be illogical, immoderate or extraordinary for the law to call on the psychiatric system.

This was the case in the Droin affair. On 5 November 1847 Marie-Madeleine Droin poisoned the little Céline Ravier, the daughter of her neighbours, with arsenic. The enquiry revealed the motive of the crime: revenge. Droin bore a grudge towards Ravier for having bought some land from her at a low price. The judiciary were struck by the disproportion between the harm caused to the accused and the crime she committed, so they requested more information and a medical investigation. This double enquiry revealed Marie-Madeleine's illness. She had lost a daughter and since her death showed signs of mental imbalance. During the six years between the death of the child and the crime she became bitter; she was aggressive towards her husband and neighbours, enjoyed seeing people suffer and wanted them to be as unhappy as she was. Witnesses also testified that she was sometimes prone to sudden attacks: she would tear her clothes, grip the curtains, hit those who tried to get near her with her fists. She would wander about the countryside, dripping with sweat, crying, looking vacant.

In prison, the doctors noticed that she avoided the company of the other inmates, made nonsensical statements and spoke to her daughter whom she thought she could see. The alienists decided that she suffered from partial melancholia. They felt that:

in all faith this woman could have murdered the young Ravier girl, giving in to unhealthy feelings of hatred and revenge, out of all proportion to the cause which motivated them. This happened as a result of the perversion of her moral sensibility and her intelligence which are the signs of partial melancholia. Therefore she is beyond the reach of the law, and her place is in an asylum.[13]

The passage from prison to asylum sometimes took place without a trial. Adèle-Pierrette, a forty-seven-year-old secondhand goods dealer, was arrested for possessing stolen goods. Her guards noticed that she was extremely odd. She pulled strange faces, she talked to herself, she had sudden fits of anger. All this revealed her unbalanced mental state. The alienists diagnosed melancholia, a form of psychosis characterized by intense depression, and confined Adèle to a mental hospital. The same fate awaited pyromaniacs and kleptomaniacs . . . but also those who claimed to be someone else.

Fictional characters

Also locked up in the asylum were those sufferers – who came to represent a stereotype of madness – people who fantasized that they were someone else. It didn't matter if they had been harmless up till then, like Rose-Henriette, committed officially in 1846. This thirty-five-year-old cook knew nothing about her own family. She sometimes claimed to be related to Napoleon and sometimes to her former employers. Dr Falret's prognosis was a pessimistic one: he foresaw imminent dementia which justified keeping her in an asylum. The case of Hersilie Rouy was even more serious. When she was released in 1863, she felt enraged against the psychiatric institution where she felt she had been arbitrarily confined, and attempted to denounce the use of special hospitals for non-therapeutic purposes. She wrote the following letter to the wife of the prefect of the department of the Seine:

> Your insane asylums have become dens of thieves where people are robbed . . . your hospitals have become abattoirs and cells where patients are subjected to insults, blows and violence by brutal and crude staff, where terror reigns, where those who complain can be locked up in dark dungeons with blocked-up windows . . . They are tortured and killed with tourniquets and showers while officials say 'to repress is to cure'. The people are displeased and when they find out that doctors draw up false certificates which are used as lettres de cachet to swallow up those who are feared or who disturb your secret houses, they will rise up and *your new Bastilles will be destroyed*.
> Signed Hersilie, sister of King Henry V[14]

The signature automatically invalidated her indictment and caused her to be immediately reinterned for five years. The instant and strong reaction by the police and the medical profession can be explained by their fear of seeing this sort of delirium develop into magnicide – the irresistible impulse to kill famous people who symbolize the authority of the state. Even when these patients did no more than 'stealing' identities in words only, or ask that their 'hallucinated identities' be recognized verbally, by actions or in writing, they were still regarded as a threat.

Their vague desires rarely went beyond these rather minor objectives. Women imagined that they were the duchesses of Berry and of Orléans, princesses, mothers of the people, multimillion-aires, the Virgin Mary, the brides of Solomon, of Napoleon, of Christ or of Abraham. Caroline claimed to be the grand-daughter of Mr de Ximènes. Anne was more ambitious – she was simul-taneously the daughter of a Polish prince, of the King of Jerusalem, the niece of Louis-Philippe, the wife of Emile or of Albert of Wurtemburg. In fact the list of character substitutes is a short one and reveals the limitations of these fictional characters. Women aspired to riches and nobility and laid claim to property and titles. They rarely gave themselves leading roles in society; if they were queens it was through marriage to a king; Colombine, 'Queen of Portugal', committed in 1846 was an exception.

The supreme ambition of madwomen was to give birth to a king: the major catalyst of female fantasies at the time was the Duchess of Berry, not as the daughter of François, King of the two Sicilies, or as wife of the second son of Charles X, but as mother of a possible heir to the throne. In their demented narcissism, the inmates surrounded themselves with the halo of sublimated motherhood. The stories they built up around the marriages their daughters would make was another form of this type of sublimation. Through these marriages, the women would gain access to the highest social classes: Justine was certain that during the winter of 1845 her daughter was going to marry the subprefect of Nantes. This made her forget her real position – a concierge married to a poor cobbler. She spent days making up the wedding gifts: 'they will be worth 20,000 francs; the dinner service will be made of gold and silver.'[15] When she was taken to the asylum, her ravings increased and she also began having visual and auditory hallucinations, in which she saw terrifying sorcerers dancing.

More rarely, the patients took on the qualities which a fictional character seemed to embody. A patient of Dr Trélat's stated her identity with pride: Henriette Constantine Hortense Venda Wasilewska, widow of Count d'Osmont of Warsaw. She explained to the doctor that Henriette meant goodness, Constantine faith, Venda wisdom and Hortense high and noble blood.[16]

Whatever fantasies they had, they remained women. Although in their madness, the inmates wanted to be someone else, they only called into question their social identity and never their biology. Only one woman thought she was Napoleon. The patients only rarely expressed regret at not being men. They didn't envy male nature but the social status of men.

Sophie, a thirty-two-year-old woman of independent means transferred on 28 May 1852 from Charenton to the Salpêtrière regretted not being a man so that 'she could obtain satisfaction by the sword for all the abuse and insults with which she is treated, for all the intrigues and machinations to which she is subjected.'[17] Could it be that the distance between the sexes was so great that even madness was unable to bridge it?

Later that century, when Jules Vallès went to Sainte-Anne he met neither Pythagoras nor the King of Mexico, but inmates 'wearing out their blue stockings chasing after emotions or glory, dreaming one day of being Clemence Isaure and the next of being Madame Bovary'; he saw committed patients 'who one day lifted up their heads out of the fog in which they were living and became saints and queens; they believed themselves sisters of the Borgias or the mistress of Christ.'[18] Madwomen saw themselves as Jupiter's daughter or his wife – with his power casting glory on to them – but they themselves never became the god.

As interesting as these cases might be in the study of female fantasies, they are not particularly important. Only the grotesque nature and not the frequency of these fictional characters explains the genesis of the popular stereotype.

Political madness

The final target of the authorities on the track of 'dangerousness' was women who had consciously or unconsciously entered the sphere of politics. In a fit of prophylactic excess, Annette, an idiot, was committed for seven months in 1853 because she wanted to speak to the emperor. Women who had attacked political men were the subjects of official committal: in 1854 Ghislaine was led to the Salpêtrière because she threw a stone at the emperor's carriage as it was going past in the street. The same fate awaited those who insulted important people.

Public violence was analysed according to the same parameters as private violence. Any political rebellion by a woman, even if it was an isolated act, even if it was mumbled in the shadows, was an act of madness. In order to silence these outbursts the police leaned on the psychiatric profession, and the latter did more than just ratify official committals and thus tacitly aid repression. The alienists did not want to remain in the wings; they thought out a theory of political insanity, thereby giving those in power scientific backing. Both parties benefited: coercion became a form of therapeutic benevolence that was difficult to attack because madness remained hidden and taboo; the special doctors left their private kingdoms, with their power and their knowledge uniting to create for them a position that was more political than medical.

But the psychiatric world wasn't homogeneous. The personality and individual approach of each doctor showed up in individual readings of 'political symptoms'. Each doctor's opinions and personal sympathies influenced the way in which the general interpretative grid was applied. These nuances can only be discerned through a careful study of each special doctor but the general tendency can be seen in the documentary evidence available. The doctors reached a consensus to refuse to see any political commitment in women as conscious, thought-out or organized rebellion. Instead, they would look to the past for an explanation of this current political insanity, which was then seen as the terminal phase of an illness which had managed to remain concealed up to that point.

Even better – or worse – alienists juggled with chronology and cancelled out past actions because of madness in the present! In September 1807, Esquirol, Pinel's disciple and the man who renewed his thought, took on Théroigne de Méricourt, who had been transferred from the Petites Maisons, as one of his cases at the Salpêtrière. Two exceptional characters were brought face to face: the man of science, key figure of the golden age of alienism, and the fallen revolutionary who was extremely agitated when she arrived at the hospital 'abusing and threatening everyone'.[19] Only a memory, by now almost a legend, was all that remained of the aggressive rebel, of the fiery feminist who dressed in riding clothes, of the beautiful Girondine from Liège. Her story was an epic which moved from Luxemburg to London, from Paris to Vienna and from Vienna to Paris, ending on the terrace of the Tuileries; on 31 May 1793 Théroigne defended Brissot to the various groups of the Convention. Shortly afterwards she was attacked by a handful of women republicans and beaten and whipped indecently. The insult apparently caused Théroigne to go mad.

She then began a totally different journey from that of the beautiful amazon. Committed at the Faubourg Saint Marceau, she was then treated at the Salpêtrière for a while. Under the Directoire she was confined at the Petites Maisons until her second transfer to the Salpêtrière. By then she had definitely sunk into madness. Théroigne no longer communicated with the world; she remained lying in her cell. She sometimes agreed to walk in the cellar but usually wandered about there on all fours with a vacant expression on her face. Her only activity was to collect morsels from the ground and eat them, rather like an animal. Esquirol saw her 'take and devour straw, feathers, dried leaves, pieces of meat covered in mud, [and drink] water from the streams when the yards are being cleaned despite the fact that this water was dirty and full of filth. She preferred this to any other drink.'

It mattered little that Théroigne's madness was subsequent to her political activity. Her madness became the essential key to analysing her political involvement. It showed that her political actions were undertaken under the influence of the illness, still latent but visible under the alienist's microscope. Her madness discredited her political activity, which was reduced for Esquirol to 'a very deplorable role'. According to him, Théroigne owed her effectiveness on the revolutionary stage to her physical charms. An alluring Eve, 'she gave herself to the various leaders of the popular party . . . and specifically, on the 5 and 6 of October 1789 she helped to corrupt the Flanders regiment.'

The doctor asserted that she took part in the October days, although no other source testified that she was present at the end of the march of Parisian women on Versailles. Some of the women convinced the soldiers not to shoot; under Esquirol's pen, this averted bloodbath became shameful and corrupt. He rubbed further salt into the wounds of the alleged degeneration of this beautiful woman from Liège. According to him, Théroigne became an object in the hands of the revolutionaries who 'took her over': 'soon she was seen with a red bonnet on her head, a sword at her side, a lance in her hand commanding an army of women.' This is clearly an exaggeration. The alienist then listened out for 'all the rumours about the amazon'. They all describe her as a perverse and morally depraved person, and reduce her to her sexual relationships.

Esquirol's interpretation went far beyond a simple case study and can take its place in the complex descriptive tableaux of the time; it needed to be quoted here because it created an inspired precedent which alienists were to apply shamelessly to the women involved in the revolution of 1848; femininity, feminism and political activism were seen as defects which would lead to abnormality and mental imbalance when combined. Political activity in women was said to be against nature. This attitude gathered so much force over the years that it became unnecessary to find other symptoms of insanity.

Initially this pseudo-scientific reading was confined mainly to the world of women; the political developments of the end of the century meant that it was more generally applied to all those who opposed the bourgeois establishment politically. The alienist Brière de Boismont did not hesitate to assert that the 'ideas which these individuals . . . have on family, property, individuality, freedom, intelligence, the structure of society are so much against nature that they can only be explained by madness.'[20]

What we are seeing here is the development of a real theory of 'politicomania', which is worth analysing even though this falls outside the chronological framework of this study. This involved analysing political activity both in terms of the symptoms of psychiatric illness, and in general medical terms. Parliamentary speeches were full of medical references: social leprosy, moral tuberculosis and mental degeneracy were invoked to explain the defeat of 1870, and this by the victors themselves! The Prussian doctor Stack perceived in the French signs of degeneracy, and asserted this even if it implied denying military glory to his fellow countrymen.[21] Sedan was the victory of a healthy mind and body over a mentally and physically gangrened body.

The French alienists didn't disagree with the essence of this analysis, but its application. For them only the common people were ill; the defeat was therefore not that of the French nation but the responsibility of a proportion of the population. To prove this they cited the Commune. Because of its specific nature and its unique occurrence, it was different from the 'traditional' revolutions of the first part of the century. Its very abnormality appealed to the alienists and a new concept was coined – demagogic madness. Brière de Boismont never stopped pointing out signs of madness in the Communards. Among the rebels, he spotted scoundrels who were not only ignorant, lazy and full of vice but also demanded immediate gratification; he also found 'failures who are arrogant, full of rage at their inability to make something of themselves, and who have sworn eternal hatred of society. There are also fanatics who dream of renewing the world in impracticable ways; these are the elements of *demagogic madness.*'[22]

Following these ideas, the special doctors created a negative image of the working class; they were seen as inevitably irresponsible in their behaviour. Unfortunately, it is impossible to know if the alienists were deliberately playing the game of the capitalist authorities, or whether they believed in the truth of their reasoning because they had access to scientific knowledge. The diatribes of some doctors like Brière de Boismont shifted from the medical to the political sphere: 'Society now knows that these sectarians want to destroy it in order to seize the estates and capital of the present owners, persuaded that they are the legitimate owners; society has the right to defend itself by all legal means against the real criminals.'[23]

According to the doctors, psychiatric institutions represented one of the means of defence to contain the epidemic of political madness. The urgency of the situation made it necessary to attack the evil at its roots and in its most acute manifestations. For these two reasons women became the target of the alienists. Calling the women fire-raisers of the Commune mad was not enough; the diagnosis did not explain how serious their case was and more detailed medical analyses were required. The alienists put forward the following explanation: women, frail creatures by their very nature, were unable to survive the psychological shock of the 1870 war; their helplessness, according to Legrand du Saulle (who had always boasted how apolitical he was), came from the fact that they found themselves with no support after the men had left for the army; and this may even have been the case before, because working-class women were the victims of the break-up of the family unit and didn't find the support they needed to maintain their mental balance. The workers, led astray by reading the newspapers, would drink all their wages in the cafés. Deprived of male moral guidance, women would immediately drift and let themselves be carried away on the wildest of tides.

This presents the fire-raisers as psychological minors, and the Commune is seen as their downfall, not their choice. It was the fall of their femininity, the time when they forgot their status as the submissive, discreet and maternal women they really were and were transformed into hybrid creatures. In the aetiological portraits of the alleged degeneration of the Communards women play a strange role. Going back to the source of the evil, the alienists discovered the traces of madness in the ancestors of the revolutionaries: the recent death of F's mother, following a strong attack of 'nerves' characterized by incoherence, aggressiveness and catalepsy, was used as the proof of F's mental imbalance.

Sometimes the heredity of insanity was traced to men, but the alienists had a strong preference for female heredity in madness. The tendency to believe that women's bodies carry unhealthy genes was particularly strong once heredity was under scrutiny. This was true whatever the nature of the illness. This genetic inferiority was not seen as the responsibility of mothers, because motherhood was seen as passive rather than active. Rather it was simply their role. Women were merely receptacles for the madness which insidiously took over female bodies in their reproductive role. Moreover, women could also be responsible for the madness of their spouses; as early as 1847 the writer Esquiros echoed this fallacious link when he asserted that: 'It is in part the fault of women if there are men on this earth who are mad, who commit suicide or who fall into the black discouragement of lunacy.'[24]

Very few alienists exposed the lack of scientific basis in this kind of analysis. In his article on 'The men and the deeds of the uprising and morbid philosophy',[25] Doctor Baume was deeply irritated by the determination with which Doctor Laborde looked for pathogenic heredity in order to reduce the Commune to a minor phenomenon. But in the concert of pseudo-scientific criticism his is only one weak dissenting voice. The shift from the medical to the political was easy to make and sometimes almost inevitable. It often happened against the will of the doctor, who became a prisoner of his own inferences. Doctor Lunier felt helpless when he became aware of the fact that the work of alienists had implications which extended beyond asylums. Legrand du Saulle became caught up in contradictions; the man who declared that he was determined to leave alienist science when politics became involved with the practice of medicine connected poverty to morality in his reports on the mental pathology of the working class. The degeneration which he diagnosed justified in his eyes being deprived of one's citizenship.

It is possible to find some resistance to the credibility science gave to this type of reactionary commentary; these were faint lines of stress within the profession. Medical interference in the political sphere was on the whole allowed at least in speech. When the Versaillais came to power, they seized on the work of the special doctors; their interpretation made the revolution appear very peculiar; it became like a short fireworks display, over almost as soon as it started, and its debris was recuperated, controlled, silenced and stifled to death. Maxime du Camp completed the smear campaign; according to him, the Commune was 'a pathological case similar to the "mal des ardens" to the "dancing epidemics", to mass possession'. The illness 'turned, after March 18th, into lucid mania, into raging dementia, into a frenzy for imitating the Jacobins, into homicidal passion, into the need for violent pleasures, into pyromania'.[26]

The writer then attacked women: 'They had thrown far more than caution to the winds, they stopped at nothing and went all the way'. In order to demolish the fire-raisers, Maxime du Camp dipped his pen in vitriol: he fulminated against those women whose aim was, according to him, 'to raise themselves above men by taking men's vices to the extreme'. He covered them in a torrent of abuse; the women involved in the Commune were described as 'evil, cowardly, deadly, drunkards, temptresses who led men astray.' Behind their demands for 'a place in the sun, citizenship and equality', du Camp saw only 'a secret dream which they shamelessly want to put into practice, the availability of many men'. Who were these revolutionary women anyway, dressed up as soldiers wearing Arab-style trousers, ready to 'overturn parliament and hang King Runt'? They were nothing more than the dregs of society, 'escaped prostitutes, scum from the slums, street vendors, "private seamstresses" for gentlemen, unconventional outfitters, personal instructors for not-so-young men, maids of *all* work, vestals of the temple of Mercury treatment and virgins of the venereal clinics'. As proof, he quoted the fact that to satisfy all its valiant soldiers, the Commune abolished prostitution: the whores, who no longer had to be checked by doctors, invaded Paris like a plague; penniless and aggressive, they went up to the front lines, 'during the last days these belligerent viragos held out behind the barricades longer than men; wherever they went crime knew no bounds.'

Du Camp regretted that the repression was so merciful, that 850 cases were withdrawn from the courts. 'Four of the women prisoners were sent to a lunatic asylum; that's too few! For someone who has studied the history of possession there is no doubt – most of those poor women who fought in the Commune were ill, according to medical science.'[27]

In this extraordinary text, we find a mixture of all the fears and all the fantasies of the bourgeois mind: their anxiety about women's demands, their terror at seeing women reject existing values, secular as well as religious ones, their obsession with a possible rebellion of 'the servant class' made all the more horrifying by the idea of it being led by a beggars' army in petticoats. Here the images of the prostitute and the bohemian merge into one picture of vice. Once again we can recognize the phobia of syphilis, which summons up the spectre of venereal disease, a physical and moral leprosy.

This astonishing synthesis is full of contradictions. Rebellious women were no longer seen as women but they became viragos who had exchanged the virtues of the weaker sex for the vices of the stronger sex. They were not women in the usual sense; they were no longer part of society but were still sexually voracious females. All their actions were seen as directed by their insatiable sexual needs; rather than just being sexual creatures, they were controlled by their sexual nature. They were no longer women, they were witches. But du Camp was a man of his time. This witchcraft was not caused by the devil, but by insanity. The women of the Commune are sick women, is the conclusion he reached in this exposé of the abnormality of the fire-raisers, their 'state of nerves . . . denoted drunkenness or hysteria'. Nothing was allowed to undermine the writer's argument, and the figure of the Red Virgin was ignored, since she was a figure who might have disturbed his anti-Communard and/or anti-female diatribe!

Four committals seem few, Maxime du Camp tells us. What conclusion can be drawn from this number? Was it that the authorities did not agree with the writer, or could it not rather be that the asylum was used by the police as one of their instruments of prevention rather than of repression, for which they preferred imprisonment or deportation? A comparison of official committals in the department of the Seine and the fluctuation of political and economic crises adds weight to the latter hypothesis. The level of committals rose before the explosion of violence. Thus, we can note that after the revolution of 1848 there was an unusual decrease in the number of committals: it fell from 7,686 admissions in 1847, to 7,341 in 1848. The figures showed a slight rise during 1849 to 7,536, and this was confirmed in 1850 (8,184 committals). The 'events' of 1870–1 also resulted in a noticeable reduction in the number of committals.

It seems therefore that asylums acted as social regulators before a crisis but this can be no more than one hypothesis among others. Since the figures we have give the development of both types of committals together, it is not possible to differentiate the role played by asylums as guardians of the social status quo, from the very real effects which political turmoil might have had on people whose mental health was precarious. The death of the insane during the revolution as specified by the alienists, and above all the fact that during periods of revolutionary upheaval the barriers between normal and abnormal are shifting, mean that it is impossible to draw any firm conclusions. Only one stands out: there was an increasing tendency to recuperate psychiatric concepts and use them for non-medical ends. The developments in the classification of diseases and the multiple ways of interpreting deviance, the involvement of both the legal and medical systems, dealt a heavy blow to the types of behaviour permitted. Freedom of behaviour was severely restricted. Above all, the authorities hunted down any possible public 'dangerousness'. Within the family a very different measure of 'normality' was current; while compulsory committals define the boundaries of what was permitted and forbidden in the public sphere, voluntary committals reveal the boundaries of what was or was not tolerated within the privacy of the family.

Outcasts from the Family

Confining conflict

For months Elisabeth kept quiet, and shut herself off in the grief she felt as a woman betrayed by her husband. But on one particular morning, after spending the night alone, waiting, she let fly with her anger and pain; in her fit of jealousy and rancour she spoke out and accused her husband of being unfaithful. He interpreted this explosion of so many accumulated frustrations as madness! Crushed, and confined behind the walls of the Salpêtrière, Elisabeth was soon restored to the submissive attitude which had been hers for so long.

At the Salpêtrière, she met Adèle. This particular deceived wife didn't stop at words to express how she felt. According to her husband, she was mad with jealousy. She showed her feelings by attacking her husband. Such violence, inconceivable in a woman, was called homicidal mania. But by no means all attempted murders were only imaginary or false interpretations by husbands. For example, Joséphine recognized that she had tried to strangle her husband while he slept; she had been driven on by a need she could not resist, which she herself didn't understand. However, no distinctions were made between her and the first two inmates.

The reasons for voluntary committals are like spotlights trained on to the intimacy of the home. This leaves in the shadows years which might have been happy and were apparently peaceful. Instead what we see are the moments of crisis and of violent tension which became impossible for women to bear. They then broke with 'normality' in a way which their families or those around them could not cope with, so that they decided to resort to committal.

The doctors and officials who backed the families invoked four types of disturbances, which were very different from the reasons for official committal. Top of the list came 'personality disorders': indifference, jealousy, fear, anger, vanity, ambition and excessive sensitivity fitted into this category. Eccentricity and various behavioural excesses such as drunkenness, suicidal behaviour, a debauched lifestyle, refusing to work and rebellious behaviour formed another group called 'behavioural disorders'. The presence of the next category in this aetiological classification is not surprising – 'intellectual disorders' basically covered reduced intelligence, hallucinations and various types of exalted behaviour.

But the last category is astonishing, since 'physical disorders' covered senility, puerperal fever, and anorexia, as well as amenorrhea and vaginal discharge. These categories unveil for us today the narrow limits of what was permitted. This was restricted further by the inevitable overlap of 'symptoms'. Where did emotional trauma stop and insane behaviour start? And what of the boundary between mental disturbance and the physical expression of those feelings? What is particularly striking is how vague these terms are. The concepts involved are so fluid that they can cover many different problems or perhaps even all situations. When did originality become eccentricity, and when did it stop being a character trait and become a psychiatric symptom?

The answer lies in the definition of female normality fixed by men and for men. Women only existed in relation to men. There were no words to describe women without relating them to men. A woman was someone else's wife, someone else's widow, mother or daughter. Nineteenth-century men repeated the saying from Genesis according to which women were created for men, and listed the 'duties' of their wives; through a clever use of words, these so-called duties were presented as female qualities. It is an endless list: it is normal for women to be generous, self-effacing, tidy, clean, submissive, charitable, devoted, modest. They were raised to the level of saints in order to be better oppressed.

It was an impossible balance to maintain, and even the smallest departure from the norm meant infringing the permitted boundaries. Women would then be said to have strayed from 'the path of virtue, which, in truth, is narrow',[1] to follow the path of debauchery. Going dancing, drinking too much (much more shameful in women than in men) and promiscuity were sometimes reasons for committal. Certificates issued outside asylums sometimes emphasized that the husband had testified to his wife's perversions. Even when it was specified that a woman was 'more perverted than insane', she could still be committed. Everything except total submission to the norm could be seen as perversion; what gave pleasure to men was madness for women. The same act could be interpreted in two ways: what was permitted to men was forbidden to women. The love affairs of young men were necessary and glorious proofs of virility, whereas for women they were the perversions of nymphomaniacs who needed treatment.

The author Ferdinand Teinturier and his contemporaries vitriolically attacked women who adopted male behaviour. For them, horse-riding, wearing men's clothes, smoking, enjoying gambling or hunting were not individual tastes but abnormal tendencies which might even be dangerous. They were possible spokes in the wheels of the well-oiled social machine. Similarly, to display one's feelings was also abnormal. Women who did this were described as madly in love, sick with pride, madly happy, wild with joy, enraged, crazy with worry. With time, these expressions have lost their meaning, but then they were seen to refer to very real disorders.

For example, take Camille, a day labourer who aspired to becoming a cook. For her partner this was inordinately ambitious. She was committed in 1850. Take Blandine, whose grief was such when she lost her daughter that she broke down, rejected her husband and refused him his conjugal rights. Or take Léonie, who was committed by her mother-in-law because she felt that she was not upset enough by the death of her husband.

They were all mad because they did too much or too little – they were too keen on studying, too emotional, too bitter, too cheerful, too pleased with themselves, too mystical . . . ; or they were not houseproud enough, not loving enough to their husbands, not attentive enough to their children. If behaviour could be categorized in this way, there were no limits to what could be labelled eccentric and therefore mad. The woman who got up at night to roam around the countryside, the woman who collected dead birds and fed them because she said that God ordered that their souls should eat, the woman who liked rain, as well as the one who hated cats, all these were committed 'voluntarily' to the Salpêtrière.

The list of what was forbidden to women is endless. They were segregated socially as well as sexually. Miss S. L, a fifty-eight-year-old spinster decided to deepen her knowledge of what she called her art. Her employers said that she was obsessed with the book she was writing on the art of cooking and by commentaries on many literary texts. When she left one job, she used her free time reading in libraries and writing – this was what she loved doing. When questioned about her lack of job stability she said: 'I didn't dislike cooking itself but the people for whom I had to cook.' Those very people brought about her committal to the Salpêtrière on 6 April 1849. There she shouted ironic quotations from Molière at the doctors.

Dr Trélat was troubled at having Miss S. L as his patient, and he questioned the soundness of the alienists' judgement.

> I had often asked myself when I passed her, and suffered the abuse which she called the 'lashes of her whip' and her 'rightful revenge', what would have happened if instead of being a cook who failed because she couldn't obey orders, Fate had made her a great lady whose right it would have been to give orders to others. Or if she had been an artist, a painter or a writer, able to create, justify and revel in her own ethical universe, while lashing the weaknesses and vices of humanity to her heart's content. Poor cook, she ended up in an asylum! She might have been the queen of a salon, fêted by all. *Could sanity and insanity be relative?*[2]

Trélat's moral scruples didn't go so far as to shake his support for the medical models of madness. Locked into the psychiatric doctrines, he kept Miss S. L in the asylum, where she died on 6 April 1854.

This kind of unease and doubt were not enough to call into question a committal. For that, far more was necessary. A subtle distinction kept Isabelle in the asylum and freed Laurence. On 17 January 1840, Isabelle was placed in Salpêtrière at her brother's request; the certificate of committal specified that when her parents spoke to her she reacted far too strongly. Her disobedience earned her two months in a 'special hospital'. Her brother then sought and obtained her release, considering, no doubt, that two months punishment would have taught her a lesson.[3]

Laurence also resisted her family. A rare case indeed, she was only seven when her father had her committed in March 1841. The external medical certificate stated that she was 'insane and epileptic'. After twenty-four hours Dr Lelut (whose patient she was) rejected the diagnosis. He suggested that she might perhaps be epileptic, but his main observation was that she had rebelled against her parents. A few days later the alienist returned her to her family.[4]

A similar 'misadventure' befell Marthe, aged eighteen, who arrived at the Salpêtrière to be treated for 'mental alienation accompanied by violence and restlessness'.[5] Two weeks later Dr

Pariset had not succeeded in finding in her the slightest trace of 'alienation' and ordered that she be discharged on 14 January 1840. Little Clémence (six), was undoubtedly the most extreme case.[6] The external doctor wasn't content merely with diagnosing her under the vague – but useful – label of 'mental alienation', but had her committed for 'dementia' at her father's request. The internal certificate noted she was 'lively, but not insane, probably badly brought up'.

A new Bastille

These voluntary committals, of little therapeutic value, suggest an astonishing similarity between imprisonment in the Bastille and committal to an asylum. Like the committals of the *ancien régime* and their 'lettres de cachet', the requests for private committal tried to protect the family. Conflict was resolved in both cases by getting rid of the troublemakers. Order was restored by putting an end to the disturbing 'debauched behaviour', be it excessive drinking, profligacy, homosexuality, promiscuity, vagrancy or a taste for gambling.

The power of the family can be measured by the silence which surrounded this abuse of asylums for repressive ends. It was only the use of the law of 1834 for police purposes which was coming under attack after 1860. It seems that only official committals had attracted attention, while the non-therapeutic elements of voluntary committals had not been noticed. For instance, Hersilie's accusations failed to mention the fact that her own official committal came after an initial voluntary committal.

Those behind this conspiracy of silence were betrayed by their vocabulary: the use of the word 'voluntary' is neither ironical nor clumsy, but accurately expresses a power relationship. To label a committal voluntary when it does not depend on the will of the person committed, and when s/he will have to wait for the decision of a stranger to be returned to society, only appears paradoxical. In reality, within the family the only will that counted was that of patriarchal power. Wives and children had to obey husbands and fathers, those beings endowed with reason. Insanity reduced everyone whatever their sex to the level of a minor and that person disappeared behind the power of the family.

The law of 1838 had given the power of taking over the right to speak for another person to everyone regardless of their sex or position within the family. The use which men and women made of this potential power is itself an indication of the division of power within family life. An analysis of the committal records (excluding the cases where the authorities substituted themselves for those really responsible for committal in cases of illiteracy) shows up the dominant role of men in the committal of women. In 80 per cent of cases the committals were requested by men. This overwhelming majority is not surprising. Nothing could be more logical than partners taking the steps they believed necessary to ensure their wives' good health. Husbands accounted for 34.7 per cent of all men putting forward women for committal at the Salpêtrière from 1839 to 1844 and 45 per cent at the asylum of Clermont-sur-Oise for the first quarter of 1848.

This percentage shows that the role of men cannot be explained entirely by the husband/wife relationship. Fathers carrying out their patriarchal duties made up 14.2 per cent of those putting women forward for committal. The remaining 51.1 per cent were other family members who were more or less distant, in-laws, male friends and even male employers. In short, the whole of male society was put into motion and the family called in all its troops, even the most distant ones, to have the (female) patient committed. For this purpose, the extended family reasserted itself and put itself forward as the guardian of the woman. This seems to have been an automatic procedure for spinsters and widows. Mentally ill widows were most often committed at the request of their sons. When sons were not involved, perhaps simply because the sick woman didn't have a son, their place was taken by close relatives (sons-in-law, brothers-in-law) or more distant relatives (distant cousins). This peculiar fact might lead us to imagine that widows never had daughters!

But who were the women who in 20 per cent of cases requested the committal of one of their own gender? They were mainly mothers: in 40.32 per cent of cases voluntary committals to the Salpêtrière were requested by mothers. They were supported by sisters and daughters. So all these requests came from women within the nuclear family. Friends only rarely intervened. It is clear then that mothers intervened, but only in particualr types of insanity, namely imbecility, idiocy, cretinism, and post-partum insanity. These illnesses fit in with specific periods of women's lives. The first three illnesses were usually congenital. The mental age of the women involved meant that they were seen as children. Therefore, mothers continued to take responsibility for them and only decided to have them committed between the ages of ten and fifteen, at the time when their role in society became more problematic. This perspective also explained the intervention of mothers who requested the committal of spinsters whose mental age meant that they would always be minors.

In cases of post-partum delirium mothers took their place alongside husbands. The fact that they were present at their daughters' confinements (which at the time were closed to almost all men) and their experience of the mysteries of childbirth meant that they were well placed to intervene immediately. But in this type of illness, the spouse also intervened rapidly because the woman's insanity, often accompanied by fever, meant that she was unable to look after the infant and obviously that she could not breastfeed. The urgency of the situation made husbands all the keener that their wives should recover their mental health as soon as possible.

This comparison proves the case. The involvement of women in the struggle against madness was restricted to traditionally female spheres. Although the law did not discriminate, it was thwarted by the hierarchy and division of power within the family. This conclusion is confirmed by the breakdown by gender of those requesting committal to the mental wards of Bicêtre hospital, which was for men only. Unlike the case of the Salpêtrière, we do not find that the overwhelming majority of requests are made by the opposite sex from that of the patient. From 1839 to 1844, 53.7 per cent of committals were requested by women and 46.3 per cent by men. True, women were dominant, but this can be explained by the role of wives; wives represented 44 per cent of men and women taken together making committal requests, but 69.5 per cent when we look at the figure for women requesting committal. Here again close family relationships bound the women making the committal request and the men who were committed. Outside these privileged relationships, women were not allowed to have men committed.

What we have seen so far about how the cards of power were dealt is significant, but it is not totally convincing because our sources are unclear. They do not take into account the role of the players who held the trump cards essential for committals – medical certificates. This means that it is difficult to identify one of the most important factors – who fathered the initial request for committal?

It was only voluntary committals for physical disorders which were clearly the result of an exclusively medical diagnosis. In other cases, the lack of archival records limits us to hypotheses.

The increase in voluntary committals gives us grounds for assuming that the resistance of families to having members committed had decreased, but this statistic could also be interpreted as the expression of the increased influence of doctors. It is likely that both these factors played a part, varying in importance according to time and place. Only one thing is certain – that a request for committal was never an anodine, disinterested, neutral action, even if we adopt the most optimistic hypothesis and assume that prejudice towards ayslums and insanity was decreasing.

In fact, literature tends to suggest very little change. Take the figure of Gervaise in Zola's *L'Assommoir*, running away from the alienist, hurtling down the street, convinced that the whole of the hospital of Sainte-Anne was at her heels, so terrified that she confused the special hospital, the doctor and Coupeau's delirium. What about the dialogue of the Pipelets, playing sado-masochistic games and trying to frighten each other before going to Bicêtre, where they thought that they would be greeted by madmen who would rush 'to the bars of the cages making horrifying noises' at the sight of a woman. They believed that there would be wardens there to calm them down 'with lashes of the whip, and by dropping down on them quantities of freezing cold water from a hundred feet up'.[7] Although these are images from fiction, they express a very real fear, that of Jules Vallès at the gates of Sainte-Anne saying fatefully, 'There it is.' He tells us that he hardly dared cross the threshold. It took all his courage to confront the 'lunatics', and he finally managed to decide to go in, 'passing my hand across my forehead . . . taking a gulp of air . . . getting my breath back and . . . going in'.[8]

The special doctors attacked these *a priori* judgements which were disastrous for their patients. Because they were so frightened, too many people arrived on the wards as emergency admissions, when their illness was far too advanced to hope for a cure or even a remission. Questioning those close to patients made it possible to identify the start of the illness, which often dated back two or three years, and sometimes more. For example, Rosine had tried to kill herself by setting herself on fire, and then by hanging. After 1841 those close to her noticed that she was getting worse, but her parents didn't feel that her behaviour was typical enough of madness, and kept her at home. Ten years later she was committed after she attempted to murder her own daughter. Another patient, Marguerite, was an extreme case. She was admitted to the hospital when she was very old, aged seventy-nine, suffering from maniacal frenzy. The first symptoms had been nineteen years earlier.

Paradoxically, those suffering from minor behavioural disturbances, ones the doctors felt might not be symptoms of insanity, were brought for committal most rapidly. Those suffering from serious disorders which led to dementia were often neglected for a long time. This difference is revealing; in the former situation, asylums were used very deliberately to get rid of troublemakers. The person requesting committal would be fully aware of the implications of their actions. The latter situation expressed the family's unconscious refusal to acknowledge the illness, since it might reflect negatively on them.

But there is one way in which we can catch a glimpse of how families were involved, separately from the influence of the doctors. We must observe the family not when the patient is committed but when she is discharged. Inmates would leave their asylums – cured, improved or in a stable condition – either on the decision of the alienist alone, or at his suggestion with the agreement of the family, or at the request of a family member. In the last case the prefect could veto the discharge. The risk that the discharged patients might carry out their threats was presented as an insurmountable obstacle and would make voluntary committal into official committal. From this point on, the person who was committed was beyond the reach of the authority of the family.

When we compare who requested committal and who requested discharge, the information makes up for the gaps in our knowledge as to who was really responsible for committals. Contrary to what we might have expected, the breakdown by gender for those who requested committal to and discharge from the Salpêtrière produces a very different picture in each case. From 1839 to 1844 discharge following the request of people outside the hospital was due to the involvement of women in 36.75 per cent of cases. They therefore played a bigger role in the discharge procedures – almost twice as many women were involved here as in the procedures for admission. At Bicêtre hospital, women were responsible for 67.8 per cent of discharges not initiated by doctors.

Therefore, the roles which men and women played did not depend only on their respective power within the family. It was also the result of the different ways in which they used the law and of their different attitudes towards insanity and asylums. These two differences are inextricably intertwined. Committal was most commonly carried out against the will of the mentally disturbed person involved. It therefore involved taking control of the situation, which was unusual for women and would inevitably lead to conflict with their husbands. The submissive stance of wives led them to accept the 'eccentricities' of the mentally ill in a more resigned way.

It was also not possible for women to be as demanding and therefore as repressive as men. The different economic positions of men and women were important factors in committals. Daughters could take over the domestic and maternal duties of mothers (taking a common-law wife was another way of replacing a sick wife!) Losing her income was not usually a great problem. By contrast, if the head of the family was committed, the family would be plunged into poverty. Thus, working-class women were more reluctant than men to resort to committal. They would turn to it if their spouse was unable to work or squandered the family's resources. Their economic situation meant that they generally requested the discharge of their husbands more frequently than the other way round.

This model did not apply to the middle class. The social position of any prominent man meant that the slightest public expression of mental imbalance was out of the question; he would rapidly be hospitalized. Private clinics offered all the discretion required by the proprieties of that milieu. Middle-class women could be treated at home for longer. They would simply be excluded from the salons which constituted their social life.

But material preoccupations do not completely explain the fact that women all tended to react in similar ways to the insane. There was another reason which affected the number of women requesting both committal and discharge. It seems to have been easier for women to cope with illness. This looks very much like the archetype of women as carers. Taking care of people was their main role, so integrated into their lives as to become a part of their nature. If they did decide to have someone committed, they would themselves follow through with the procedures to the end. They would not hand over their responsibilities to others or lose interest in the fate of the man or woman they had had committed. Women who requested committals also took on the responsibility of getting patients released from the asylum. They appeared to believe in the therapeutic nature of asylums more than men. Women seemed to give themselves a certain amount of time to test whether the asylum had a therapeutic effect. After this time had elapsed, they called for the patient's return to the family regardless of whether there had been any improvement. For men, asylums seemed to act more as places that would take in the sick women they themselves could not or would not take care of. Once relieved of their burden, men showed little concern, if any, with the fate of the inmates. Women's feelings seemed to stand up more to the trials of madness and confinement.

When women did not think that asylums offered the possibility of improvement, they rejected them. They found it difficult to accept the committal of members of their family. Instead they preferred to take on not only the trials of living with madness, but also the financial burden that it represented. There are numerous cases in which inmates committed by their father are freed after a short stay in hospital by their mother's intervention. Only when they were driven by poverty did women agree to be separated from a member of their family. Therefore the increased number of requests for committal by women from 1843 to 1844 were premonitory signs of the crisis of 1845.

The fact that it was so often women who requested discharge from asylums confirms the fact that asylums were sometimes used by men to silence women. The discrepancy in numbers we have just discussed hides more than one domestic tragedy.

Mothers, sisters and daughters came to the rescue of female members of their family whom they felt had been wrongly committed. They either refused to believe that the person was mad, or they did not see committal as a solution and preferred to take care of the sick person within the family. This interpretation is not the wishful thinking of sisterhood, wanting to present women inmates as victims of male tyranny. We have evidence that a good number of release certificates took into account this split within families. It was not uncommon for a doctor who had taken in a woman at her husband's request to return her (according to the wording used then) to her mother or her aunt. He often justified his choice by saying that these women relatives were prepared to take on looking after the madwoman, who had 'improved' but was not cured. But there were also many cases when, after a brief stay in an asylum had allowed doctors to observe women who had been committed, they decided to free the women in question because they were not mad. These women did not go back to the marital home or to the men who had had them committed. They fled from their persecutors to take refuge with other women rather than with another member of their family.

Equality in the eyes of the law came out as inequality in practice, as we have seen, given the division of ideological and economic power within society, and the different attitudes towards madness and asylums. The way in which the law was

used depended very much on the person using it. It allowed men
to use the asylum as a place for treatment but also as a means of
relieving themselves of the worry of having a sick woman on their
hands. It was also used as a way of preventing women from acting
outside the accepted norms of behaviour, and showing opposition.
Asylums served as places both where women could be imprisoned
and where they would be forgotten.

If confinement was a solution which came easily to men, it was
by contrast one which women would adopt only in extreme
situations and which they saw as provisional. But both men and
women resorted to it when they felt that the behaviour of a family
member endangered the sacred institution of the family. The
Revolution denounced state secrets (used to justify imprisonment
in the Bastille) but family secrets still flourished. The sick family
member was a victim of the way in which so-called normal
behaviour was defined as the type of behaviour society allowed.
Rejected by the family body, s/he left the family unit for another
unit . . .

From rumour to scandal: two parallel lives

The procedures of voluntary committal often opened the doors of
individual homes to reveal family conflicts. No sooner glimpsed
through a discreetly half-open door, they would disappear again
because one of the protagonists would be committed. From then
on the conflict could only be seen through the complaints of some
patients or their refusal to see their partners, now described as
'loathsome murderers'. These cries have been muffled by the high
walls of the asylums, poorly described in inadequate sources and
distorted by those who wrote about them. Historians trying to
find out more become frustrated. They would like to be able to
uncover daily life in all its small, banal details, but have to settle
for less, to leave behind the details of daily life and delve into the
sensationalist stories available. They have to give up the hope of
telling the stories which have never been told and study the ones
which have been told too often. Two of these stories would be on
the front page of today's gutter press with sensationalist headlines
like 'The Packard case' or 'Rouy'.

What Elisabeth Packard, confined at Jacksonville in 1864, and
Hersilie Rouy had in common was their refusal to give in, before,
during and after their voluntary committal. When they were
freed, they both started lawsuits against the asylums and the men

who had had them committed. Compared to the medical world which is secretive and silent, the legal world thrives on words. There were investigations and cross-examinations to shed all possible light on both these 'case' brought before the courts. For the historian, frustrated up till then at being able only to glimpse shadowy figures of women inmates, this is a godsend. And because female madness is similar everywhere, a historian can go outside France for more information on the subject.

Because it is a focus of attention, madness is a constant in the study of mass psychology. Although the way it is perceived varies according to the prevailing socio-cultural climate, there are common attitudes to madness throughout our Judeo-Christian civilization. This might tempt us to see the mind as autonomous and ahistorical. This is not the case but we can still look at it in a wider historical context. Female madness relates to concepts of femininity, of being female. This means that there is nothing to stop us from using the experiences of female inmates of different nationalities alongside French sources. Although the legal climate, the non-medical reasons for committal and the political context in other countries make up a framework different from that in France, the experience of asylum life is international. There is a psychological and physiological similarity in reactions to life in the asylum. In mind and body, female inmates are women first and foremost, and only then Americans or Frenchwomen through their education and culture.

THE PACKARD AFFAIR

Elisabeth Packard lived in Manteno, in the county of Kankakee in Illinois. She was the wife of the Calvinist minister Theophilus Packard with whom she had six children. At her husband's request, Elisabeth was confined in the asylum of Jacksonville. It was an arbitrary committal. On 18 January 1864, an Illinois jury acknowledged that she was not mad.

Yet for nearly twenty years the couple had seemed completely united. Elisabeth had been brought up in the same faith as her husband and helped him in his parish duties. But in 1859 the household fell apart over religious differences. When she was asked about the influence of the Christian versus the 'sinner's' attitude towards their respective financial profits, she answered from the pulpit that financial success was not linked to religious attitudes. 'Losses and profits, dollars and cents are currencies which have no value in the spiritual world, the opposite of true happiness and suffering.' For Elisabeth 'the true rewards of piety [are] enjoying a greater sum of happiness.'[9] The reverend father, a rigid and cold man, was infuriated by the stance his wife had taken.

The *Kankakee Gazette* of 21 January 1864 painted a grim portrait of him, 'a cruel husband, a ruthless torturer, a ferocious little saint who always looked cold and threatening', before describing him as a tyrant: 'Pursued by his own guilty conscience, seeing that his wife was about to escape from his clutches and that a cloud of indignation was about to burst on his head and be unleashed mercilessly on him, he left the area at great speed, with the mark of infamy on his forehead.'[10]

Beyond his bombastic manner of speaking, there was no denying that Mr Packard was an intolerant man who tried to have his wife confined to an asylum to break her opposition to him. On the other hand, the testimony of doctors, neighbours and friends all agreed that this forty-four-year-old woman was intelligent, even though they might share her husband's opinions. These thumbnail sketches are enough for us to guess the kinds of clashes which can arise when two such different temperaments meet. The storm burst when Elisabeth came out of the shadows, proclaimed her own opinions loud and clear and committed the crime of thinking differently from her husband. This provoked her spouse's anger and he set himself up as a judge/god/protector and saviour figure.

The laws of Illinois stated the following: 'Married women and children who in the opinion of the medical officer are clearly insane or mentally disturbed can be committed or detained at the request of the husband, of the wife or of the child's guardian, without the proofs of madness required in other cases.'[11] This was a godsend for the Reverend Packard; he claimed that he was acting for the good of his wife to save her soul from complete depravity. He wanted to 'make her normal'. Elisabeth didn't see things in the same light:

> My husband, sir, do I not have the right to my own opinions?
>
> Yes, you have the right to have your own opinions *if you think correctly*.
>
> But does the constitution not defend the right of each American citizen to his own opinion?
>
> Yes, it defends that right for each citizen. But you are not a citizen; *as a married woman, you have no value, you are not even a person*

before the law. In short you do not exist legally given that you are a married woman.[12]

This dialogue contains the main elements around which Mr Packard structured his argument that Elisabeth was mad. Her madness was expressed by a religious stance which was not in accordance with Calvinism. She therefore showed signs of religious mania, an attitude which was itself part of the list of types of deviant behaviour. But through her husband's words we can see that she was considered mad not only because she had wrong opinions but because she had opinions at all. Mr Packard combined religious, medical, moral and legal excuses so that he could do what he needed to save her soul . . . even though legally she had no soul. These short cuts didn't embarrass him in the slightest; he used all the means available to reduce his wife to silence, and morality, politics, religion and medicine did their utmost to support this spiritual murder.

Their religious conflict was the catalyst for a more fundamental opposition. By taking up the position she did, Elisabeth defied her husband and the ecclesiastical power structures which he represented. Consequently, both the theological rigidity of the reverend father and his intolerant attitude were backed and supported by the Presbyterian community as well as by his own family. Elisabeth's brother-in-law said of her: 'She would not have left the [Prestbyterian] Church unless she was mad.'[13]

Those who spoke against her were not worried by the fact that she was not the only person to hold the religious views she did – in fact her beliefs were close to those of the Methodists. This is proof that the theological problems are only a pretext. One of the witnesses, Sarah Rumsey, said while she was being cross-examined: 'What was mad about her behaviour in my opinion was that she continued to defend her ideas. I don't know if there are many people who think the same way as she does, but what I do know is that a lot of people don't think that the Calvinist doctrine is the right one and that doesn't make them mad.'[14]

Perhaps her religious madness hid another form of insanity. And because Elisabeth didn't give up – which led to her being labelled as incurable after her stay in the asylum – all her actions were looked at through the prism of her alleged madness: 'distraught, strange, overexcited, manic' . . . the witnesses speaking against her described her in terms which could belong to the novels of Eugène Sue. Her clashes with her husband meant that she was 'overexcited', and seemed 'very disturbed'.[15] Her grief at her husband's attitude made her seem strange: 'her voice, her way of speaking, everything proved she was mad',[16] as did her anger and her resentment:

> On another occasion, at the dinner table, she was talking about religion and Mr Packard reprimanded her; she answered in an irritated way that she would say what she wanted to say and when she wanted to. She got up, took her cup of tea and left the room violently.[17]

Elisabeth's reaction to her husband's unshakable hostility was to rebel even more; she no longer confined herself to theological debates. The nightmare existence which her husband put her through led her to criticize the whole condition of married women. She claimed the status of a human being, the right to have a separate legal existence, to bring up her children according to her own principles. When she was released from the asylum, she became a militant feminist, spoke out for all oppressed people be they women, psychiatric patients or blacks. Her theological rebellion changed into a rebellion against patriarchy. She had come to understand its power through her father, her husband and her doctors, and she refused to give in to it.

> I want my father to understand that his daughter is of age and able to live without depending on her father's money or according to his authority . . . Why should I thank my husband for giving me back my own inalienable rights, my children, if this will cost me my own identity?[18]

Elisabeth stopped saying thank you, because she had understood that she was 'a pioneer who was twenty-five years ahead of her contemporaries and as a consequence [she was] seen as eccentric, mentally disturbed, completely mad.'[19]

THE ROUY AFFAIR

Hersilie Rouy was confined for fifteen years in French special hospitals, first under the voluntary committal procedure then under compulsory committal, before her confinement was declared arbitrary. In 1854 Miss Rouy was admitted to Charenton at the request of her half-brother Daniel. He used the asylum to rob her of her inheritance. To be safe he hid behind the committal doctor,

Dr Pelletan. The external certificate of 8 September 1854 stated that the patient suffered from 'acute monomania with hallucinations, which make her a danger to herself and to others'. The doors of the asylum closed on Hersilie. From Charenton to the Salpêtrière, then from the Salpêtrière to the regional asylums, she never stopped complaining that she was being held illegally. When she had finally escaped from the psychiatric world, unrecognizable and aged by all she had been through, she used her last remaining strength to regain her moral integrity after getting back her freedom.

She was not satisfied with the 1868 certificate that ordered her release. It stated that, given her relative calm, and despite a few eccentricities, she could be returned to society. It also stated that there had been a just reason for her confinement. This ex-inmate then sued the Assistance Publique. In the final section of the trial she partly won her case. The report of Counsellor Crisenoy admitted that 'Miss Rouy was a talented artist' who kept herself by her work. Her confinement was said to be illegal because the doctor who approved her committal was also the person who requested it, and this was against legal regulations. Moreover, the doctor had seen her only briefly, and judged her mental condition from the hearsay of her neighbours.

So why was she mad in their eyes? It was because of how she lived; she was a spinster who earned her own living, an artist who lived from her talent and always wanted to develop her artistic skills further. She was a single woman who enjoyed her solitude and shut herself off in her apartment away from people and noise. All this was a sign of abnormality which her neighbours underlined, amplified and offered up on a silver platter to her family and to the doctor who was her spokesman as reasons why she should be committed. All this is important because 'medically, the certificate itself relies only on the reports of concierges and the rumours repeated by third parties.'[20] As in the case of Elisabeth, there was a shocking gap between the actions seen as symptoms of madness and the allegedly therapeutic measures taken. This gap unveils the violence of the established order, and the strength of the discriminatory social norms then in existence.

The lives of these two women were ruined because they both refused to fit into the roles assigned to women, and wanted to live their lives as men around them lived. What did they suffer from, these two women? It seems that they were madly intelligent, madly ambitious, madly independent (or wanted to be so), madly rebellious. They were exceptional characters. The nameless women of the Salpêtrière were not heroines: the similarity between those women is their joyless past, and the misery of their present lives in the asylum. From these similarities we can draw up an identikit picture of the madwoman.

3

THE IDENTIKIT PICTURE OF
THE MADWOMAN

Were women physiologically susceptible to madness?

It seems that at certain times in their lives women were more likely
to become mentally ill. The statistics for age at committal show an
increase at three different times: at fifteen, at thirty to thirty-five
and at fifty. These figures speak for themselves and suggest that
we should see the picture not in terms of age, but in terms of three
periods. The inmates were either newly pubescent girls, or young
mothers, or women who had just gone through the menopause.
Doctors classified women according to the stage they had reached
in this biological calendar. This breakdown of women's lives into
specific stages was established in the medical dictionaries; the
entry for 'woman in the famous Panckoucke distinguished
between: 'pre-puberty, puberty, post-intercourse, the state of
pregnancy, the moment of giving birth, the post-natal period, the
period of lactation, the end of menstruation, the post-menopause.'[1]

This division of women's lives did not remain only a medical
view but became widespread; it was, however, toned down and
the emphasis was put on motherhood as a time when women
blossomed. The fact that these ideas were so common means that
women must have taken on this concept of their lives as having a
set rhythm. The way in which they approached these physiological
watersheds was to a large extent the result of the socio-cultural
context in which these physical transformations were explained
to them – or not explained as the case might be. The two most
powerful moments in this reading of women's lives were puberty
and the menopause, and they were reflected in the asylum
population.

PUBERTY

There was a complex relationship between puberty and madness, which was above all a social one. Puberty was the time when girls were thrown from the world of children into the world of adults, in other words from the world of innocence and protection into the world of responsibility and sociability. Those who were mad, or more often mentally handicapped, were able to survive in the world of childhood. Whether or not their parents wanted to keep them they certainly had to because there were very few measures taken to deal with mad children. Through the efforts of the alienists Félix Voisin, Onasime Seguin and Hippolyte Vallée, a few shortlived schools were set up. Sometimes attempts were made to send 'idiots and imbeciles' to centres in the countryside. This was only on a very small scale; in 1846 only sixteen children were involved. It was only in the middle of the century that wards for children were set up at Bicêtre and at the Salpêtrière. The mental weaknesses of mentally retarded young women, their inability to distinguish between good and evil, made them easy prey for unscrupulous men. Their parents often saw asylums as a way to protect them against catastrophic pregnancies.

There were also medical reasons for the committal of young girls of thirteen to fifteen. It cannot be denied that during puberty latent or minor illnesses appeared or developed. In this category we can include the worsening of congenital idiocy. But puberty was not only an aggravating factor, it also seems itself to have caused mental imbalance. The ravings of the young inmates often concerned blood and things associated with it – the colour red, wounds. In listening to these patients, we can hear what a major trauma menstrual periods were for them. They spoke about how disgusted they were by menstrual flow, and this feeling of disgust spread to their whole body which they felt was decaying. For them, this process of decay was a punishment from God, but strangely, rather than seeking purifying water they were afraid of it.

These first experiences of menstruation were common to most young women, the reflection of contemporary habits and customs but taken to extremes. Puberty was only glorified when it was assimilated to potential motherhood. But this glorification was done by a small number of scientists who knew the role of menstruation in reproduction. General opinion continued to transmit a negative image. Periods were seen as an illness, a wound; this unclean blood stained women, who were already incapacitated by the disability of menstruation.

There are striking similarities between the attitude to menstruation of these madwomen and the women from the village of Minot in the Côte-d'Or questioned in 1980 by Yvonne Verdier, an anthropologist. They also felt that they were locked into a biological destiny that was mysterious, shameful and frightening. 'Apparently if we could see into a woman's body at that time it would be horrible, a real mess, all upside down; it can't be described in words.'[2]

The madwomen experienced periods as an internal tempest. As the onset of menstruation grew closer, we can understand the effect it must have had on the imagination of young girls.

In cases of amenorrhea, the relationship between madness and menstruation are clear. The psychological causes for amenorrhea are well known today and the menstrual cycle has always been sensitive to such pressures. Amenorrhea affected mostly girls who had just reached puberty, perhaps because of their fear of the biological tempest that was about to burst. Some of the inmates expressed their fear by saying, 'I don't want to bleed.' Unfortunately, confidences of this kind are too infrequent to allow us to make further generalizations.

THE MENOPAUSE

Menstruation comes . . . and goes. There is a link between puberty and the menopause. The age at which menstruation stops is 'from 35 to 40' for about one-eighth of all women, 'from 40 to 45' for about a quarter, and 'from 45 to 50' for about half and 'from 50 to 55' for about one-eighth.[3] The dominance of the forty-five to fifty age group is reflected in committals, except for idiots. Otherwise all women, rich and poor, suffer the same physical degeneracy: 'When the desires of nature are fulfilled, women gradually lose their bloom, and the delicate flowers around which all gathered. All men then disappear like the morning dew.'[4]

The menopausal woman was deposed from her glorifying maternal function, and the ultimate aim of her existence disappeared. She also lost her sexuality. Current opinion then believed that when menstruation stopped so did sexual relationships. This conception of the menopause followed a more general view of sexuality. Women only had a sexual life in their reproductive role; therefore it was impossible to assume that they would still be sexual after menstruation had stopped. To do that would be to recognize that women had their own sexuality which was independent of their reproductive role, and this would mean admitting the existence of female sexual desire and pleasure.

At the moment of the menopause, women were the victims of sexual taboos which hid behind medical jargon. Having lost their role as 'childbearers' they were now 'useless to the world'.[5]

The nineteenth century is not famous for its kindness towards the aged, and old women were particularly badly treated. Even if they were sometimes revered as mothers, they never had the aura of the old man whose years give him wisdom. The menopause made women shadows of the shadows which they already were 'by nature'. 'A critical period' was the accepted way of describing the menopause in less medical terms. This vocabulary and the way in which it was used at all levels of society underlines the way that women took on this analysis of a biological phenomenon which they experienced themselves, but which was defined by male discourse.

This meant that menopausal women joined pubescent young women in their anxiety about the menstrual cycle. It is paradoxical that totally opposite situations could put women in a position where they felt that they had failed, because of the appearance or non-appearance of menstrual blood. The paradox is more apparent than real, because once women had come to terms with the shame of having periods, they gained the power of giving life and of organizing that life within the home. This power was limited, but real nonetheless. Women held on to it and pinned on to it all their hopes and desires. The menopause therefore took away from women the only power they had.

This makes it clear why the ending of menstruation caused depressions which went as far as 'lypemania', a melancholic depressive state, and why women in the fifty to seventy age group were less affected by age-related fluctuations in the numbers of committals, up to 1845. After that date the increase which took place reflected a specific political attitude towards asylum which gave a crucial role to marital status. Whatever the marital status of women, the menopause was a traumatic event: the point at which periods ceased put an end to childbearing, both for women who already had children and for those who wanted them. The latter had to face the fact that they had failed irrevocably, and this was the case for spinsters who had missed their destiny as mothers. They were the ones whose despair was deepest. They refused to acccpt their new biological status, which also involved a new social status, and this sometimes led to deliriums which centred around the subject of pregnancy. Unfortunately for us they most often expressed themselves by becoming mute. The relationship between the menopause and madness seems to have been closer than that between puberty and mental illness.

Women over sixty stood out from the larger group of post-menopausal women. There was a very strong connection between age and committal in this age group. We can go so far as to assert that age was often the reason for committal. Official committal drained off a whole population of old women who were unable to carry out their daily tasks because of their reduced intellect. Asylums acted as old people's homes. Both minor disturbances (such as loss of memory and reduced intelligence) or major ones (such as senility) were made psychiatric issues. In most cases old women were voluntarily committed, involving the family rather than doctors who, as we have seen, complained about the assimilation of age and madness. They condemned the easy choice many families made and their refusal to take responsibility for their old relatives.

The way in which old age gradually became a psychiatric problem was not only ideological but also reflected material problems. Doctors rarely returned these old madwomen to their families; when they asserted that they were not insane, the doctors passed them on to the paupers' wards, just as they tried to do for old women who had been officially committed.

It is very difficult to separate biological and social factors in this area because the two are so closely related. This problem arises much less in the third important period in women's lives: motherhood.

CHILDBIRTH AND MADNESS

Women were frequently committed after childbirth. Post-partum insanity was more frequent after the first delivery and explains the high number of committals of women between twenty and thirty. These women were suffering either from intense depression or acute frenzy. The period of insanity was usually short, followed either by a rapid remission or by death. The frequency of these cases, particularly the more serious ones, can be linked to puerperal fever which was very common. These cases will be excluded from our discussion because of their physiological basis.

The silence of the mothers means that it is not possible to find out whether the birth of the child was experienced as a 'loss of the object' and could explain these mental disturbances. We therefore have to make do with this brief outline of post-partum insanity, and emphasize the fact that it was more frequent than today is linked to puerperal fever caused by the unhygienic conditions in which women gave birth.

What conclusion can we reach about the links between madness and these critical moments in women's lives? It seems that at these moments women were made to feel more vulnerable, because biological factors alone (hormonal balance) cannot explain the neurological disturbances which affected them. Women felt very apprehensive when these critical moments drew close, particularly puberty and the menopause. These explosions of mental disturbances related to physiology did decrease. This is because physiological facts were made less dramatic when women began to know more about their bodies. The taboos which made these physical transformations mysterious and therefore frightening began to break down and society gradually began to accept these physiological facts as normal. These changes emphasize after the event what a crucial role culture played in the development of neurological disorders.

Madness and marital status

Family status was closely linked to age; there was a time to be young and a time to take on the natural role of women and become a wife and mother, devoted body and soul to her family. To move into the next age bracket without taking up the corresponding family status was itself seen as abnormal.

SPINSTERS

The percentage of unmarried women at the Salpêtrière was close to 50 per cent. This proportion was all the more overwhelming given that it was not reflected by a high level of single women in the population as a whole; only 30 per cent of women over fifty were unmarried in 1841. In Paris, where the influx of men from the countryside had affected the gender balance, single women were sought after by the rootless men desperate to have a family. The arrival of servants who were usually unmarried increased the percentage of women in the population of Paris, from 49.6 per cent in 1841 to 50.98 per cent in 1851, but this did not yet mean that there were too many women, statistically unable to find husbands. The situation was reversed in the countryside where the rural exodus decimated the group of possible husbands and as many as 50 per cent of women were spinsters.

In the asylums statistics were subject to a rigid vocabulary. Sophie-Françoise was an 'unmarried woman' of thirty-three, committed on 1 October 1839 on Dr Pariset's ward. A few days later the doctor wrote to her 'husband' to 'take her back'.

Pauline's case illustrates a second kind of misunderstanding. This single woman of thirty-eight was committed to the Salpêtrière at her daughter's request. The single mother and common-law wife was a reality of daily life but these women had no legal existence, although from 1837 to 1847 one-third of all births were illegitimate! The word 'unmarried' therefore included all women who were neither married nor widows; it covered all long-term common-law wives, as well as those women who just spent small parts of their lives with temporary partners; it included unmarried mothers and lonely spinsters.

Despite this lack of precision one thing is certain – there was a higher proportion of unmarried women inside asylums than outside. They made up 40 per cent of voluntary committals to the Salpêtrière between 1838 and 1848, against only 28 per cent of official admissions. This is an astonishing proportion given that unmarried women were by definition solitary beings. Their position in society explains this apparent discrepancy; single women had to earn their own living. This meant that they were out of their homes more than housewives and could be labelled 'mad' by colleagues or employers as soon as they saw the slightest signs of madness. Mental imbalance and employment were incompatible, and employers could become the ones who requested committal. More often they would simply sack their mentally ill employees, since they didn't care about the women's future.

The situation was different for domestic servants who were single on principle. The bourgeoisie would not accept the slightest trace of abnormality at its very heart. Since every gesture they made was watched, these women who worked were unable to hide their mental difficulties for very long. At this time, the spread of a phobia of syphilis linked venereal disease and madness in the mind of the bourgeoisie, and this meant that mentally ill servants had to go immediately. The bourgeois lady who requested the voluntary committal of her maids in an asylum – since this task fell on women's shoulders – was doing her duty in two ways: as a keeper of the sacred hearth she was protecting her home, and as a philanthropic mistress she was kindly looking after the welfare of her employees.

Madness made it impossible to work. Single women who were ill had no resources to fall back on. Their situation was much worse than that of married women, and their single status played a crucial role in this. If they lived alone, insane unmarried women were no longer able to pay their rent and they would be committed at the request of their landlords, often described by the word 'logeur'. If there were noisy outward signs of mental disturbance, the porter of the block would intervene as spokesman for neighbours who preferred to hide by remaining anonymous.

Although as spinsters women didn't have their own families, they were often integrated – in appearance at least – into someone else's home. This is the familiar figure of the spinster taken in by a charitable relative (a more or less close family member), symbolized for ever by the figure of Cousine Bette, Balzac's eponymous heroine, reduced to being a lady's companion.

More or less accepted by society, spinsters who became mentally ill became embarrassing – financially if their mental illness meant that they were not able to work, but also morally because their presence was a stain on the family, disturbed it with their symptoms and raised the constant problem of 'dangerousness'. In short they became too heavy a burden to take on. The temptation of asylums as a solution was the more difficult to resist because there was not such a close emotional tie as between a married couple. Nephews or brothers-in-law would therefore carry out the procedures necessary for committal. There were also frequent cases of committals by elderly fathers. In these 'couples' it was the role of the unmarried daughter to stay with her father and look after him until he died. These fathers were unable to reverse the roles and look after their mentally ill daughters.

So the anomalies in the committal of unmarried women were not an indication of privilege but of the exact opposite, rejection.

Being an unmarried single woman therefore meant an increased likelihood of being committed. But could it also have been favourable ground for mental illness? This is what dictionaries of the time asserted; they gave spinsterhood as one of the causes of madness. When we listen to what the spinsters within the asylums have to say about their state, their emotional and mental loneliness stands out in their plaintive murmurings or sporadic screams. These were brief but poignant expressions of their feelings as they cursed the emotional emptiness of their lives which made them go over the edge. Too much hope and too much despair in love destroyed these women. As early as 1842 Dr Dulaure pointed to love as being one of the causes of madness. In his study he quoted the cases of thirty-seven men for whom love and madness were closely linked. Although it is not always specified, there are heavy hints that this love with a capital L was both emotional and physical. A hundred and sixty-six single women were also mad through love, like the woman from Alsace at Sainte Anne who went mad with love for a dustman.[6] Her love was thwarted and she didn't go mad because of too much passion but because her passions remained unsatisifed, because of a frustration more emotional and mental than physical.

Lucie's mind was not able to bear being 'misled by a married man who said he was single',[7] and she went into a state of dementia which led her to the Salpêtrière in 1843. The trauma was such that it led to her death. Her doctors unfortunately did not specify her age. Noémie B sank into lypemania, which was rapidly diagnosed as incurable, because of the 'coldness of a young man'[8] of forty-nine! Ernestine, a woman of fifty whom solitude had made 'sour and jealous' was seized with a fit of madness when her niece's engagement was announced. She threw herself on the young woman, and tried to strangle her, screaming 'he's mine.'[9] These reactions are surprising both because of how frequently they occurred and how strong they were. They prove not only that women invest everything in the loved one, but also that they were unable to compensate in any way. Without Him, they felt that they had no existence of their own or that they had never lived. A proof of this is in the family fictions made up by spinsters in asylums.

A fantasy husband was a constant creation in these neurotic constructions; single women wanted to be wives and by inventing husbands filled a gap. But this was probably not a case of sexual frustration as suggested in the Greek etymology given by the dictionaries of the time for the word 'celibacy': '*coïté*, bed, coitus, and *leipo*, I lack: I lack the bed where coitus takes place.'[10] Or at least, if frustration there was, it did not seem to lead to a specific type of pathological behaviour. Unmarried women were not accused of onanism any more than their (married) fellow inmates. What unmarried women were refusing by their madness was a particular marital status. Without a husband it was said women remained children. This is how the scientists of the time spoke and one of them, Virey, asserted that 'women remain like children because they are deprived of sperm.' Married women, according to him, are more confident and bolder than 'shy and delicate virgins'.[11]

So, getting married was a way for young women to gain access to womanhood and to begin to exist in their own right. Although even then they would only exist by proxy because, as the Panckoucke dictionary explained, women 'cannot exist in their own right and are forced to use the people around them to strengthen their own lives'.[12] This denial of the existence of unmarried women which makes them half-people must have been internalized by women who were shaped since their childhood by the hope of getting married. As the years went by and made them into spinsters they became increasingly worried: 'Why don't you arrange for me to be married?' writes Jeanne to her father, 'I may be ugly but I am the right age. And after that: *omnia vasa operculum habunt aut inveniunt.* Consequently, I should not despair. But it is time. My grey hairs might begin to show. So, soon, father, I don't want to die an old maid.'[13]

This state of spinsterhood which already frightened Jeanne (she was twenty-two years old) was believed to become a physical defect. According to popular proverbs Jeanne knew that her skin would turn yellow and dry up, and she would become as masculine as a prostitute. Unmarried madwomen therefore threw themselves into an unequal struggle against time; they were excessively conscious of their appearance, visibly worried about their attractiveness, which was essential if they were to make the conquest of a husband, the only conquest they wanted to make.

Their anxiety was similar to that of girls who had been raped. The extent of the trauma caused to these inmates aged between fifteen and twenty was less a result of the blow to their physical and emotional integrity than a consequence of the weight of the moral blemish. The inevitable shame of rape made marriage impossible whether or not the victims were pregnant. In the Shorter Dictionary of Medical Science, Esquirol emphasized this aspect of rape which could make the victims, 'both chaste and soiled', go mad: 'I have seen some young girls who, after being raped, lost their mind; shame and sorrow were the real causes of their illness.'[14] Madness was therefore a consequence of society's judgement rather than of the act itself. So the madness caused by rape affected young women more than wives who protected themselves by remaining silent.

These feelings of guilt about an act of which they were after all only the victims conflicted with the analysis of the statistics of rape as a cause of madness. Muteness is one of the clinical symptoms of raped women who were committed, but the position given to rape by doctors in their table of causes underlined its importance in the development of mental illness. Moreover, guilt seems to have been present even when the sexual relations were desired. Remorse can become unbearable. Geneviève, who had stayed a virgin until the age of thirty-eight, then met a woman, who, according to her, 'introduced her to dangerous secrets'. Two years later she confided to the doctor the remorse which drove her mad.

> Since she lost her purity, she would pray and cry without ever finding comfort; she felt that she was aflame, it was as if her 'soul was in a furnace'. Often it would tell her: you are in control, you will not die. Now her eyes are dry, her heart feels nothing, she is damned, she is immortal. She walks in the streets of the hospital slowly and unsteadily, she looks gaunt, she looks dazed rather than in pain, telling whoever will listen to her the punishment inflicted upon her. 'No one will believe me when I say I am immortal,' she often repeats; 'people think that I say that because I'm ill; but no, I'm not ill, I don't feel anything any longer. If it was only a thought I could say it would stop, and when I died people would be able to see in my head what gave me these ideas. I would be really happy if it were only ideas. A stone or marble figure is immortal, but I am a living immortal statue.'[15]

Neither society nor religion offered single women compensations. Spinsters were excluded both from the family and from an essentially male society. They were not validated in the world of work; their role there was negated, as much by the philosophers as by the proletariat. For the positivists, women could have no individual effect on society, and could therefore not be respected 'for her personal qualities outside the family circle'.[16] The depreciation of women's work by the predominantly male workforce had a more material basis; out of a gut-level fear of competition, working men recommended to the conference at Marseilles in 1879 that their female workmates should return to their homes and families.

As for the Church, it only celebrated celibacy within its own confines. Even this was pretence; in fact nuns were married to God, and only existed by and through Him. Outside the Church unmarried women were outsiders who were not carrying out the divine plan.

This denial of their existence made the situation of unmarried women even worse, and created favourable conditions for mental disturbances to take shape, given that women needed poles of reference from which they could work out their position in society and structure their personality in relation to the role they were given. Paltry alternative solutions did save some of them from this frustrating situation. Being servants offered a kind of home; married to their masters and living only for them, they saw themselves as full members of the family. These escape routes were limited . . . but madness on the contrary was a limitless escape. Reality was hidden by the mental world which the insane created.

The religious monomania which many single women showed was a variant on their matrimonial monomania. In their mystic fervour, madwomen proclaimed far and wide that they were married to God. Adopting current religious terminology made it possible for these patients to feel less lonely, but they didn't emphasize having offered up their virginity to God. Some stated that they were married when they were admitted to hospital, and doctors only amended their marital status later when they understood that their patients were in fact 'married to God'.

But marriage alone was often not enough for self-recognition; as Stéphane Michaud pointed out, 'the fact that women were excluded went hand in hand with a sort of curse which could only be lifted by motherhood.'[17]

Public opinion was therefore unanimous in seeing women primarily as potential mothers; to be single was an unnatural state, in a Rousseauist conception of nature which turned women into mothers. Indeed Virey tried to make the word 'femme' into the basis of this kind of philosophy. He claimed that the root 'fœmina' came from 'fœtare' and 'fœtus'. Hey presto, if you were not a mother, you were not a woman.

The fantasies of single women who had been committed reflected the hold of this indoctrination. In their frenzy, they invented children so that they could pour out the surplus of tenderness which they felt on to a rag which played the part of the baby, and thus fill what Madame Necker called 'this terrible emptiness'. The same fantasies are found in 'imbeciles'. Marie-Rose, aged thirty-three, was committed in 1841 at her mother's request on the grounds of madness. Dr Falret diagnosed congenital imbecility, and in his second certificate he specified: 'She has become infatuated with the idea that she has had relations with a man and that she had several children, in circumstances which were quite clearly untrue.'[18]

Apart from the common family fictions – common in their structure and in the frequency with which they recurred – there were a few unusual variants of the maternal role. In their frenzy, unmarried madwomen believed themselves to be the mothers of France, of the Fatherland, of Justice or of the Church. The object of their fixation was clearly motherhood rather than children themselves. The impossibility of achieving the ideals for which they had struggled in vain led them to sublimate birth itself. This fantasy motherhood was full of honour and glory.

Pregnancy and childbirth in the fantasy world of inmates were not painless. The stomach was clearly the privileged place in the body for somatizations of mental states. Noémie complained of violent pains in the bowels which as the 'mother of the Church' she attributed to the 'synod which was taking place in her stomach'.[19] This may have been a way of expressing the biblical line 'you will bring forth your children in pain and suffering', which was also expressed by their intermittent fits, modelled on the pains of women in childbirth; in many cases the wish to punish themselves can also be seen in the patients. They condemned themselves to suffer because the fact that they had not borne children was perceived as being ungrateful towards society.

Unmarried mothers had an ambiguous position. Their feeling of self-worth was increased because they were mothers, but they were rejected by society for having conceived a child while unmarried. The feelings of guilt won out in the case of mentally unstable women. And the unmarried mothers of the Salpêtrière denied that they were mothers, refused to recognize their sad 'situation' and the existence of children which the fathers and society also refused to recognize. Marguerite's doctor believed that her feelings of shame at the birth of her daughter were the reason for her madness. She wanted to wipe out her transgression by planning to commit suicide after throwing her daughter out of the window so that she at least could escape the evils which life had in store.

Flaubert's Félicité (in *Un coeur simple*, A simple soul)[20] symbolizes these deeply disturbed unmarried women; she sums up their behaviour. she who is, by her Christian name, the incarnation of happiness was unable to find happiness, unable to imitate, parrot-like, normal female behaviour. She substituted imaginary constructs born of her own mental confusion for the normal elements of the everyday life of women (marriage, motherhood, family). She lived by proxy through her mistress, she behaved towards her parrot Loulou like a mother, but Loulou was also a man, the Holy Spirit to whom she was devoted. These three types of monomania in her story, related to the family, to motherhood and to religion, became intertwined to make 'a simple soul' into mad felicity.

WIVES

The implication of the strong link between being unmarried and being mad was that marriage was a position which gave status and security within society. It is precisely because of this equation – marriage = psychological security – that madness in married women was so odd. Most of the mental disturbances in married women were caused by calling into question this framework. Family problems are top of the list of the so-called moral causes for mental illness in married women; the physical causes belong mainly to the famous line 'after childbirth'.

The adjective 'domestic' sets the scene for the madness of married women within the home. It seems to have been more difficult for women to deal with the problems which might threaten to break up the family unit, their only frame of reference. The distress caused by any crisis within the family led to great feelings of confusion. For the women who were the most mentally vulnerable this led to mental disturbances which would finally end in committal.

Three different kinds of situation could threaten the home and the wife's mental balance: a deterioration in her relationship with her husband, change within the family, or a threat to the socio-economic unit which the family constituted. For example, Charlotte's marriage was unhappy, and her despair about this made her lypemanic. She only came out of her muteness to complain about her husband's lack of attention to her. Justine would talk to her husband for hours, pretending that he was with her to try to re-establish their relationship, putting forward the most outlandish suggestions. If she were a bird, would he love her more?

This brings to mind Emma Bovary who was disillusioned by her marriage and whose adulterous liaisons did not succeed in compensating for her disappointment, so that she sank into deep suicidal despair. This was obviously fiction, but doctors did refer to the heroine of Flaubert's novel in diagnosis and described this kind of neurotic behaviour as 'bovarysme'. The extent of the confusion of unhappily married women was proportionate to how much they had invested emotionally in marriage.

An unfaithful spouse could be a fatal blow for the precarious mental balance of some women. Inmates often mentioned adultery to explain the onset of their madness, and the story of their lives was divided into two periods - before and after the betrayal. In their frenzy, they cursed the unfaithful husband who had ruined them, rather than the other women. Women had far more difficulty in dealing with adultery than men. Doctors saw this as an expression of the natural jealousy of women. They obviously hadn't listened to the disjointed words of their patients.

The reassembled fragments which are all we have today of these women's cries suggest something very different. What irritated and traumatised women was not so much the fact that the affection which was their due in the marriage contract was given to another, as the possibility that the marriage might break up. Although the wife's adultery might lead to a break-up, it didn't plunge a man into an inferior social position, even though 'the cuckold and the man who had been left' were figures of fun. When a man left his wife, she became an 'abandoned woman', and this would define her from then on in the eyes of society.

Adultery implied the threat of a break-up and was enough to create states of anxiety which led to serious psychological disturbances. It is easy to understand how actually being abandoned acted as the catalyst which could cause women of fragile psychological health to go over the edge. When they arrived at the Salpêtrière there are innumerable Melanies who had sunk into mental illness after their husbands had left them. Some only emerged from their prostrated state to call for their unfaithful spouses, others refused to recognize the painful reality – in their frenzy, they reunited the separated couple and talked to their spouse. Some found excuses for their absence: in their madness they imagined that their husbands were travelling or at war. These madwomen were not only less passive but also less downcast than their fellow inmates who were in the same situation; it was easier to bear the husband's absence, even in a tragic context like war, than his desertion, which called the wife herself into question.

This self-questioning was changed by the abandoned wives into self-blame. They believed that they were themselves responsible for the departure of their spouses because they didn't know how to 'keep' them. If their husbands had left, it was because they had shown themselves unable to make their husbands happy. For many of them happiness meant making a welcoming home.

Marguerite accused herself of the 'crime' of being a bad housewife. Many of these women tried to blot out the sin which haunted them. They spent their days cleaning; they constantly carried out the daily actions of a housewife; they were obsessed by cleanliness and wanted to wash all the time. The meaning of this word which they repeated over and over again was unclear. Washing means cleaning the house, but it also means washing away reality, as well as figuratively cleansing themselves . . . of the shame of having failed at their duty, and of being abandoned. They wanted to wipe out the stain which would mark their life for ever.

Strangely enough, some inmates would destroy their work. Camille spent her days folding up the few clothes she had, then a violent phase took over and she energetically tried to tear up her bodice, then all her clothes, and she would have done so if the hospital staff had not intervened. This sequence of behaviour was often repeated, expressing despair or rebellion.

These feelings of guilt clearly expressed the fact that women had internalized the model of the good wife at home which society was gradually setting up. Marthe in Zola's *La Conquête de Plassans* admits to Father Faujas: 'This is not a confession, I'm telling you my sin. After the children, I let the father go and he never even hit me, poor man! I was the one who was mad!'[21]

The insanity of abandoned wives was built on their internalization of their own domestic servitude. Their neurotic and psychotic constructions were built on their terror of finding themselves alone in mental and financial destitution.

MADNESS AND THE BREAKDOWN OF THE FAMILY UNIT

The origins of the madness of widows were twofold. It occurred as much because of the loss of a loved one as because of the loss of mental and financial support. These impoverished widows joined the crowd of 'paupers without means' and the doctor summed up their personal tragedies as 'a state of poverty after the husband's death'.

Another form of disruption in the family unit was the death of a child. We don't need statistics to see the impact of this loss on the mental health of mothers. The mother who went mad following her child's death has become an archetype which is still present in the collective memory of our age and remains topical today. The mother mad with grief is a symbolic figure, and is frequently represented in the visual arts.[22] The commentary on the reproduction of Gavarni's work *A Mad Mother* in *Le magasin pittoresque* dissects the mother's madness and explains what it consists of. Her mental balance was shattered by the death of the child, but in this case madness is not presented as yet another trial: 'God who had taken away her child has had pity on the poor mother; she is now mad.'[23]

Although the actual experience of madness is the epitome of horror, it is portrayed here as a present from God; madness made it possible for the mother to believe that her child was still alive. She would not be able to live without this illusion because 'the child completes the mother's life.'[24] Madness is the only possible course which would make it possible to continue to live. The mother lived through the feelings of love created by the 'presence' of her child, which even hid the walls of the asylum:

> When the wind whispers in her cell, she thinks she is hearing the sound of her child breathing; when the sun's rays shine on the stone wall, she thinks she sees his smile; when a bold bird pecks at the crumbs near the bars of her window and chirps away, she listens with delight to her son's first words.[25]

There was such a close link between cause and effect (the death of the child and the mother's madness) that there was no need to introduce an organic cause of madness. This is proved by observing the madwomen born in the imagination of writers, but who are so close to the real inmates. They can regain their senses when the cause of their madness disappears. This rather theatrical twist in the plot brought back from madness both the recluse of Notre-Dame de Paris and Marie Stoub, one of Balzac's characters from *L'Israélite*, in a state of frenzy since the presumed death of her son, who becomes sane again when he turns out to be alive.

All these women, real or imaginary, were not primarily wives or unmarried women but above all mothers, and all had similar experiences. They were so frightened of their children dying and their psychological equilibrium was threatened to such an extent that the possibility of death was enough to bring about mental disturbances. The common expression 'mad with worry' applied particularly to mothers. Angeline went mad after her son's illness; Berthe became a lypemaniac because of her worries about her son's fevers.

The mothers of men who were called up were also mad with worry; war endangered 'the flesh of their flesh'. Eugénie went mad when she learned that her son had been picked to go off to fight; conversely, Marie-Joséphine's sanity gave way at the joy of learning that her son had 'drawn a lucky number'. From Dr Dulaure's study in 1824 it was noticed that war had different effects on the sexes. Thirty-five women were so terrified by the Napoleonic wars that they went mad. They were not frightened for themselves but for their children who had become cannon fodder. Men, on the other hand, seemed to sublimate their feelings by doing their military duty. War did not make them go mad; it only led twenty-one men to simulate madness to escape conscription.

Once again, the patients' feelings of guilt featured in their clinical records. These feelings play as large a role in the genesis of madness as the pain of loss itself. Emilie inflicted the same fate on herself as her child had suffered because she felt responsible. Her son fell into the fire. Not only was she terrified but her husband also blamed her for not being watchful enough. Emilie went mad and deliberately burned her hand. She repeated this action as often as she was able to. The hospital staff were able to watch her and save her from herself.

These feelings of personal guilt usually led to less spectacular punishments: often they didn't go beyond being 'wishes' or pleas from the frenzied women. They wanted to be judged, punished, killed, or saw themselves as monsters. This self-punishment also operated on the level of the unconscious. Because they believed that they had failed in their duty as wives and mothers, the inmates rejected their femininity in somatic disorders which were far fron neutral, and included amenorrhea and inhibited lactation.

Their attempts at suicide were less a desperate quest for death as the end of their suffering than a punishment to wash away the shame of having failed in their duty as mothers.

The final danger threatening the family was the economic breakdown of the family unit. In the catalogue of causes of madness, doctors often included this in the category of 'domestic problems', whereas financial setbacks are put in a different category for men. When this is included in the portrait of the pathology of inmates, as it is in Dulaure's, it only came sixth in the list of causes, as against taking third place in the study of the growth of madness in men.[26]

What women feared was poverty for their children. The fear of not being able to keep them sometimes caused mental disturbances. Some of these were even preventitive. These women were 'peniaphobic', that is obsessively frightened of poverty, and they were obsessed with collecting and keeping food. This terror of poverty meant that their husbands' ruin might lead to a breakdown. The death of a partner seen in terms of economic disaster was the reason for the madness of some wives. But this was only one of the components in the development of madness, which is more often related to the patient's age and her professional status.

Women, madness and social and professional status

The complaints of the unhappily-married women of the Salpêtrière were a muffled but pathetic echo of the wails of Madame Bovary. And there ends the analogy between the inmates and Flaubert's heroine. Idleness was not their problem, as 46 per cent of the inmates committed in Paris in 1845 were working women. The group of women without a trade was made up of women of low intelligence and older women whose illness had become too advanced. This latter group, who were judged to be hopeless cases, were the first to be transferred to the provinces. The Salpêtrière's records draw a picture of traditional women's work in the capital; the patients were mainly manual workers primarily in the clothing trade – seamstresses, linen maids, laundresses. They might also have practised one of the other activities which flourished in Paris, like furniture making, where they might have been illuminators, varnishers, polishers, upholsterers or wood gilders.

They also did the various small jobs which the capital created; those who were pedlars, or who sold souvenirs and rosaries, were on the lowest levels in the world of work. There was only a small distance between them and paupers. At the other end of the scale the shopkeepers, who were more often than not essential supports to their husbands, and a few primary school teachers were not numerous enough to lift up the economic and socio-cultural levels of the asylums. The only distinguishing feature of the professional make-up of the Salpêtrière was the overwhelming majority of seamstresses and linen maids.

The partial explanation of the doctors would now make us laugh. They believed that the vibration of the sewing machines affected 'non-cerebral organs'. This new version of the 'wandering womb' theory smacks of prejudice. Sewing machines were only just being introduced and the most common tool was still the hands; moreover, this explanation disregards the equally strong presence of laundresses. It is quite likely that these stated occupations in fact hid other activities too shameful to mention: until 1845 prostitutes stand out by their absence on the registers of the Salpêtrière. Besides, in people's minds, laundresses and seamstresses were often seen in the same light as prostitutes. This was the reputation of laundresses near rivers; their morals were said to have been 'affected by their constant contact with mariners, and dockers'.[27] Seamstresses were said to be similarly affected, sitting behind the counter looking at men passing by, choosing their next lover. These were cover jobs, but which, as time went by, fooled no one. Prostitutes affected by the increase in official admission from 1846 preferred silence to this clumsy camouflage. From that date there was a massive increase in the proportion of inmates whose profession was not given.

No specific pathology for specific trades can be deduced from the clinical records. It is impossible to trace potential correlations between the growth of industrialization and madness in Paris. At the time the capital was not becoming heavily industrialized, unlike northern France. There, chronic illnesses were more frequent; the occurrence of total paralysis, of epilepsy and of idiocy were much higher than ever found in the south. Was this a result of industrialization? The doctors answered that it was, but one of them, Dr Foville, criticized the consequences of factories rather than factory working itself: social life was focused around taverns and they were also open to women; the link which developed between factories and madness was alcoholism.

So any possible connection in Paris between madness and work lay in other areas. The numbers of paupers who were impoverished working women, the frequency with which the word 'debt' recurred in the restricted vocabulary of inmates and careful attention to their 'ramblings' reveals that it was not the nature of work which led to psychological disturbances but it was the loss of a job or the possibility of losing it. The population of the asylums reflected the effects on the poor of low pay and dread about the future.

Amongst these impoverished inmates was Marie, a widow and the mother of four children, who had scraped a living doing embroidery. When work became scarce the whole family was plunged into poverty and Marie became a melancholic. The doctors noted these 'effects of poverty' as a primary contributing factor to her illness. This is supported by the statistics available. At times of economic crisis, as the factories emptied, the asylums filled up. Dictionaries made this fact official by giving pauperism as a cause of madness. But it was easy to generalize a little too fast; poverty was often the straw that broke the camel's back for women who already had a lot to contend with. Wasn't Marie's illness as much a result of being a widow and being alone as being poor? Madeleine's illness was caused by her difficult past: she had an illegitimate child and was then abandoned by the father, who ran off with her savings. She then fell into pauperism and went mad, 'as a result of poverty' according to the doctors.

The threat of poverty also implicitly affected mental health. When churches closed, the mental balance of women who sold rosaries was shaken; the seasonal nature of seamstresses' work meant that in June and October the rate of committal of women from this trade increased. The spectre of poverty distorted reality and made small incidents appear bigger than they really were. In many cases losing a valuable possession was experienced as an irreplaceable, priceless financial loss. Losing her purse was the final straw which made Fabienne go mad – she who had survived being raped, and as a consequence being pregnant, and the death of her child.

There is no doubt that objects had a symbolic value as can be seen in the disproportionate attachment of inmates to their rings, but their value was not only symbolic. In their 'fits' many patients talked about their terror of poverty. They frequently personalized it and this led to paranoia, when the madwomen thought that they were being persecuted by poverty and dying from its effects.

The fear of poverty – whether real or potential – often went hand in hand with self-blame. Women saw themselves as responsible for the desperate plight of their family, and saw debts as punishments for their inability to manage their budgets. The wives of ruined tradesmen behaved in the same way. They saw the bankruptcy of the business as their own failure and it ended years of struggle and hope. They rarely rejected their husbands; when they did, the husband was seen as a spendthrift and the reason for bankruptcy as his drunkenness and debauchery rather than the social and economic context.

For women, therefore, work was only a shield against poverty, which was shameful, dramatic and their fault. They only took account of the 'nourishing' aspect of work, probably because it was up to them to stock the cupboards and to fill the family's stomachs. This link with food and fear of running out were constantly found in the inmates' speech; madwomen desperately stocked food not for themselves but for the family left behind at a bare table. If there was no food they treasured dried leaves, earth or snails which they imagined to be food.

Having to work in order to survive made it difficult to be personally committed to one's job. The ideal washerwoman was described in the popular song by the German, Adalbert of Chamisso (1839);[28] her life was mapped out by God. She was a devoted wife and mother, who cherished her home. When she was widowed, she worked to feed her children, to bring them up as honest, good citizens who worked hard. This great task over, she had only one aim left: to save a small sum with which to buy some linen for her shroud which she sewed herself.

This makes it clear how different the relationships were between male and female insanity and work. Out of the 43.5 per cent of women committed in France from 1856 to 1860 for so-called 'moral reasons', only 9.4 per cent were admitted for a work-related cause, as against 26.24 per cent of men. Within this category 'too much mental work' led to 44 women as against 314 men being interned, grief over loss of money affected 296 women and 550 men, frustrated ambitions led to 296 women being committed as against 364 men, and moving from full employment to retirement affected 19 women and 63 men.

It was rare for women to be professionally ambitious; Marie-Pauline and Elisabeth were exceptional cases, but their background showed them to be already suspect. The former wanted to embroider the Queen's dress, and the latter wanted to transform her small business into a vast shop like the new department stores. Only artists seemed able to sublimate their feelings within their actvities. This is significant. Being an artist presupposes being able to find fulfilment in one's talent; the hope of glory comes before money and artists have a different relationship with their profession from those working in other areas. Being an artist was not at the time seen as a profession, particularly not for a woman. Hersilie Rouy was a pianist and spent her time at piano lessons, rehearsals and concerts; her references to her profession and her gifts triggered off sarcastic comments from her doctor who had no compunction in writing under the heading 'profession': 'she claims to be a musician'.

Women from the country who arrived in Paris had no great feelings of ambition or desires for sublimation. They simply wanted a better life. Paris rarely lived up to their hopes as they had to face the combined problems of being uprooted from their homes and economic difficulties. Their geographical origin was not a factor in the development of their illness, but in fact underlined the presence of inmates from all the border provinces in Parisian asylums. It was the timing of their committals which was striking.

There were two particularly difficult times for the newcomers to go through. The first was the initial uprooting and the second taking stock of what they had achieved. The more fragile women would show symptoms of madness in the few months following their arrival. After two years, the mental disturbances linked to this rural exodus faded away. They did not die out completely, but flared up again after ten years, this time even stronger, more appalling and with less hope of a cure. These women seemed to have given themselves a fixed period of time to build up their social position; when the period came to an end, if they had not achieved their aims, their mental equilibrium, already shaken by years of struggle and difficulties, collapsed completely.

As soon as they had made some improvement, these inmates from the country rejected Paris so strongly that they dared to take the initiative themselves, a very rare feat, and suggested to their doctors that they should return to their village. The doctors were aware that the transition from the world of the asylum, where life was relatively easy, to a teeming and constantly changing city was very dangerous, but despite their requests, patients were very rarely helped to return home. After 1845 these patients tended more often to leave Paris. They benefited indirectly from a measure which was only aimed at combating the overcrowding of hospitals in Paris. The Bureau Central sent patients back to the province from which they had come, calling it their 'normal home'. They would still be ill when they left and they would need to be rehabilitated and reintegrated into village life. This was not dealt with by Parisian asylums and no information is available about the fate of these women.

The identikit picture of the madwoman which we have drawn in this chapter shows a woman on her own, financially and/or emotionally, and more often than not at a biological and therefore a social turning point. The wide difference between cases makes it a shadowy picture. Patients in the special hospitals were from the lower classes of society, for demographic and economic reasons, not because of any therapeutic ones. This distorts the picture and makes it seem as if the lower classes are madder. Nevertheless, women of private means and women who were property owners made up 7 per cent of inmates in France from 1856 to 1860. This is a big percentage given the proportion of women in this group. It is even weightier when we consider the number of silent cases. Madness among the bourgeoisie was treated at home: in 1866 there were 58,687 mentally ill people of both sexes in their families, including 18,734 who were insane and 35,973 idiots. Those who had the means could also be committed to private clinics, often under deliberately misleading diagnoses.

More than finding similar traits which can be used to draw an identikit picture, studying these shattered lives reveals identical crises and points of reference. What these women had in common was the way in which their lives had gone off the rails. This was because of socio-cultural factors, which all revolve around the family, rather than biological factors. Female madness was born and was experienced within the home to which women were attached like nuns to their community, on the margins of the social developments and upheavals of the time. This is in contrast to male madness which was very much a product and an experience rooted in the current historical events.

An identikit picture of madness?

Madness – like madwomen themselves – takes on different forms and it is difficult to try to define it precisely. It is not possible to generalize about madness. But we can say that in order to escape from a reality which they found unbearable, nineteenth-century women used all the mental escape routes which the psyche could provide. They did not restrict themselves to one type of insanity. The way in which we glimpse the specific nature of female mental disturbances is by looking at the nuances of behaviour and by comparing the illnesses of women and men.

The originality of woman monomaniacs lay in their choice of the object of their frenzy. The fantasies of the inmates focused on religion: at the hospital of Saint-Yon of Rouen, 37 per cent of the disturbances of the inmates were caused by religion. The level to which women were involved in the Church can be measured by the extent of mental disturbances when any changes occurred in the existing religious structures which they used as reference points for their own stability. When churches were closed in 1830, many regular female churchgoers reacted by states of anxiety which went as far as madness. The ideology of the 1848 revolution was accompanied by an increase in the committal of women for religious monomania: in their ravings, these women wanted to achieve Peace through the Church.

RELIGIOUS FRENZY

Female religious monomania was centred around three dominant themes: religious persecution, religious practice and communication with divine or evil powers. For Marie, Pauline and Thérèse, religion was terrifying. All three imagined that they were being hounded by God's representatives. Marie, aged fifty-six, wrote to the authorities to complain that she was being persecuted by the Jesuits. She was a nurse who travelled dressed as a nun and tried to found a nursing home near Dijon. Ruined and hunted down, she was arrested by the police and committed in November 1865.[29]

Pauline's ravings had a similar theme: she did not wear a nun's habit without being entitled to, but wanted to be admitted to the Sacré Coeur. The culprit was here again a cleric: the parish priest of the church of the Trinity was supposed to have taken from her 6,000 francs, her dowry for the convent. Her complaints to the prefect led her to the Salpêtrière in September 1865.[30] The monomania of Thérèse, aged thirty-one, was less detailed: she thought she was being poisoned by a nun, an obsession accompanied by olfactory and gustatory hallucinations. The tormentors were very rarely women; usually these fantasy persecutors were men, devils or abstract concepts such as electricity, an obsession with raving lunatics.

Cases of monomania with religious excesses were more frequent and less spectacular. Convinced that God wanted them to take part in austere practices to allow their souls to enter paradise, these madwomen would spend hours in prayer and never leave the church. Ernestine was such a case. She wanted to take communion every day. These women would accuse themselves of every sin or were convinced that they were responsible for all the misfortunes of the world for having failed to do their duty; Esthel thought that God punished the whole of humanity as a revenge for her adultery.

These 'sinners' would punish themselves so that God would forgive them and above all so that he would spare the rest of humanity; they stepped up their religious fervour and, guided by auditory hallucinations, they refused to eat. So religious mania and anorexia went hand in hand. Self-blame was therefore a trait common to many madwomen regardless of the form which their madness took; this was not found in the records of men's wards. It is possible to interpret this *mea culpa* as the internalization of the interpretation of the diatribes of priests who, from the pulpit or in the secret of the confessional, repeated the same message: 'Woman, primary source of sin and death . . . you who manufactured all the evils of the world.'[31]

Freethinkers accused priests of stealing wives from their husbands. Religion certainly filled emotional gaps. More often than not a painful experience, it sometimes became the origin of sensual rather than metaphysical pleasure, as in the case of a patient of Dr Leuret. She thought she could see God and would kneel in the sun; she

> would then feel internally elevated, and experience extreme pleasure. God was speaking to her. The pleasure she felt was experienced particularly strongly in the chest and stomach. God, she said, can make us feel raptures everywhere, in all our limbs. She saw him not only when she saw the sun, but in the dormitory, on a walk. She only needed to pray in order to see him.[32]

This last category of religious monomania relates to mystical experience. The patients posited the existence of non-material forces. They were prey to auditory hallucinations, sometimes also to visual ones where tones of gold were dominant, and would then experience visions of the redemption, announcing the arrival of the Messiah. God granted them supernatural and beneficial powers. Jeanne, a day labourer, claimed that through her prayers she would be able to cure the entire world and use her fortune to cover Paris with gold. The small woman with gentle features and big, tender eyes whom Jules Vallès met at Sainte-Anne was awaited by the Archangel Michael at the Academy[33] and the patient demanded to be allowed out soon so as not to keep the saint waiting!

The divine powers who inspired these patients gave them the task not of reforming the Church but of setting France to rights. In the dispute between supporters of the Bourbons and the Orléans kings, God would entrust to these women the task of ensuring that the right king (who varied depending on the inmate) should be recognized. The recurrence of the legend of Joan of Arc, which was favoured by the political context, is striking.

Once the royalist crisis was over, madwomen put down their pilgrims' staffs which had defended royal justice. Religion and politics remained intertwined but in a less repetitive way. In their altruistic frenzy, madwomen gave themselves the roles of distinguished advisers to political leaders; thus Elisa wanted to explain to Napoleon III the political position to adopt to fight the poverty which she had experienced herself. It is striking that these inmates, with a few rare exceptions, were on the side of those in power; they never questioned the government of the day; they were not revolutionaries and had great trust in governments because of the prestige of their authority.

If governments acted badly it was because someone was misleading them – 'they are misleading you', 'they are fooling you'. The inmates were there to help. They were the ones who denounced the evildoers who were deceiving the king, and showed him the truth. This type of behaviour is reminiscent of the people for whom Louis XVI was a good king who had been led astray by the lies of the aristocracy. This similarity in the reading of the politico-economic situation is astonishing, given the revolutionary times which the country had known since 1789. Might it express the fact that these women were strongly attached to traditional structures and accepted established power because its charisma gave it validity?

MADNESS AND SADNESS

Fear, terror and dread were the feelings which gripped these women. Once their periods of violent agitation were over, they sank into silence and sadness became the dominant symptom of their madness. It was also the first symptom of madness which many of the inmates showed. There was a striking contrast between the clichés repeated *ad nauseam* by alienists, doctors, philosophers and all types of writers and the reality of asylums. One one side was a picture of Racine's Hermione – 'Venus toute entière à sa proie attachée' – madwomen seen as agitated to the point of convulsions, portrayed as aggressive, shamelessly and uncontrollably sexual. The other side of the picture was Emptiness – madwomen in asylums were prostrate and despondent. They had no appetites, no voice and no periods. This was the experience of over a third of the inmates during the years 1838 to 1860, the golden age of alienist medicine.

There was a particular type of madness which from the time of Esquirol onwards was seen as separate from monomania and called lypemania. After mania and monomania, it was the third most common of the curable mental illnesses to lead to committal in an asylum regardless of the sex of the patient. But above all there was a privileged link between this type of disturbance and the female sex. More than one-third of women inmates in asylums were affected by lypemania, while for men the proportion was not so high, and the gender gap increased with time.

However, when he separated lypemania from monomania Esquirol did not underline the specific link which the statistics reveal between this type of mental illness and women. On the contrary he considered that women were not often subject to lypemania because of their capricious nature; this meant, for him, that they were less likely to become totally involved in any activity the failure of which would act as a catalyst for states of anxiety which would lead to lypemania. When the development of statistics seemed to contradict Esquirol's theories, the doctors changed their tack. Although Girard de Cailleux noted the privileged link between lypemania and women, and Calmeil pointed it out in the Medical Dictionary, thus making official the link between women and lypemania, their analysis repeated, by a sleight of hand in which these doctors were expert, the arguments which Esquirol himself had used to prove the opposite point. This time it was argued that women were weak and that their weakness led them to invest too much of themselves, unwisely, in an activity whose failure disillusioned them and affected their mental health.

In fact, women most often became lypemanic after the sort of emotional losses which we have already studied. This cause and effect relationship suggests that when they 'chose' lypemania, women were transposing on to the psychological level the emptiness of their daily lives. In this way they were indeed 'the rich who had become poor', but this expression of Esquirol's takes on a different meaning in this context; these women never even belonged to themselves but to others. It was losing the Other which plunged them into lypemania. So their illness expressed more than discomfort with their existence. It expressed the possibility that they, together with their nineteenth-century sisters, had no existence in their own right – they were mothers, wives but not women . . .

When female lypemaniacs broke their silence, the little they said was an attempt to recreate the situation which had existed before the trauma which had led them to the asylum. Yet it all preserved the dramatic theme of guilt and unworthiness. Even in these cases, the break with reality was only rarely accompanied by violence. Women suffering from lypemania needed to be controlled by being confined in cells far less than men, although the number of male sufferers was numerically and proportionately much higher. Female lypemaniacs therefore privileged certain features of the disease, namely depression, mutism and self-blame; they only rarely showed the suicidal tendencies which were far more common in men. Women did not contribute to the increase in the suicide rate in Europe. Without reducing suicide to its socio-cultural elements only, these are crucial in our attempts to understand why attempted suicide was less common in women. Although efforts were made to make suicide a medical condition, it remained a shameful act, self-murder and therefore – in accordance with the Judeo-Christian tradition – a crime against God. It was therefore a mortal sin but also a crime against the laws of society. Although the legal status of suicide changed (prosecutions stopped in 1810), society's attitudes changed very little and suicide remained shameful for the person who had committed or attempted suicide, and for his or her family.

Looked at from this point of view, the low level of suicide among women can be interpreted as the consequence of the fact that women had internalized to a very high degree what was or was not socially permitted. Their rejection of self-harm was reinforced by the feeling of maternal duty which led to a greater sense of responsibility for children and the family unit. The ability to cope with difficulties which is often put forward as an explanation for the low level of suicide in women is on the whole a result of this internalization of their inferior status, of the 'suffer in silence' attitude. Lypemania was thus a compromise between real death, which was forbidden, and normal life, which had become unbearable.

Therefore, the privileged link between lypemania and women was less about the instrinsic nature of women than about their social position, and more specifically about the relationship between women and violence permitted by nineteenth-century society. Psychoanalysis asserted that the violence which is latent in all human beings is much better controlled in women than in men. But this was more because women had resigned themselves to following the rigid social code of the society in which they lived, than because they were determined to control their aggressive and morbid impulses.

When Adélaïde, an old widow of seventy-two, could no longer bear her constant terrors, she stopped her plaintive moans and tried to kill herself by drowning in the Seine. Justine threw

herself down the stairs and Jeanne chose asphyxiation. Female
suicides chose more discreet and passive methods of suicide than
the violent methods men used – firearms or hanging. The
brutality which Clémence showed when she threw herself into
the fire was unusual.

Contemporary literature noted this gap and made it into an
archetype. The Rubempré type (after Balzac's hero), who was a
victim of spleen – an attenuated and fictional form of lypemania –
managed to end his life. But melancholic heroines were rarely
allowed to commit suicide actively. Although they were allowed
to fade away like Madame de Mortsaulf in *Le Lys dans la vallée*,
they were rarely active in seeking death.

So, in their search for death as in the forms their madness took,
women were passive: they took refuge in silent madness or killed
themselves secretly. The true idiosyncracy of female behaviour
was to be passive, and this is the constant, the key to the repertoire
of behaviours of madwomen.

On the other hand, hysteria was not defined in psychiatry. It
was everywhere and nowhere because it was impossible to define.
'A protean figure with as many colours as a chameleon',[34] it could
not be clearly categorized. This annoyed the alienists, and doctors
like Lasègue were in despair, convinced that 'there never has
been and never will be a definition of hysteria.'[35] In the records, it
is found only as a symptom, describing an illness but very rarely
defining it. Danielle was committed in October 1846 for nervous
hysterical incidents; she was kept there in July for hysterical
madness; four years later she was called a lypemaniac.

Female madness was defined by the forms it took on the whole,
but also by the forms it did not take. It very rarely followed 'abuse
of alcohol'. Escaping through alcohol was a male behaviour pattern.
Was this because the café was essentially a place for men or
because of the social attitudes which devalued alcoholic women
more than men? The two factors were closely tied, and the taboo
against women drinking appeared again and again in the efforts
which dipsomaniacs made to repress the strong, sudden and
apparently unmotivated urges which drove them to drink and
which occurred in waves. One of Dr Trélat's patients could find
no other guard against drunkenness than to mix excrement with
her wine, and she abused herself: 'Drink, you wretch, you drunk-
ard, drink you wicked woman, you are neglecting your duty and
shaming your family.'[36]

Marie behaved in the same way; her medical records tell us
that:

This poor woman would drink all the alcohol she could lay her hands on . . . but there seemed to be two people in her, one who was good and one who was evil, and the former would punish the latter. When she was taking the alcoholic drinks, she would always reproach herself bitterly and abuse herself. She even went as far as putting earth, cinders and faeces in the wine to make it unpleasant and off-putting.[37]

When she was about seventy-two, Marie was cured of her dipsomania, but the doctors judged that her sanity was fragile and, since she had no means of support, she was not allowed to leave the asylum and spent the rest of her life there.

Part II

ENDINGS

LIFE IN THE ASYLUM

First impressions

When what had begun as peculiar behaviour had become unbalanced behaviour and the reaction had changed from a lack of comprehension to rejection, from restriction to repression, madwomen were taken away from their families or off the streets into asylums.

Small cracks in their sanity had become deep chasms and they were subsequently seen as 'only good for Charenton' or the asylum at Bailleul. They were fit to 'follow the Boulevard Boulle', which led to the asylum of Marseilles. Because the available medical records are very nearly silent on the subject, we know very little about how they reacted to being torn away from their daily lives and to the brutal separation from their families which committal to the asylum entailed. Apparently, Josépha tried to escape by throwing herself down the stairs, Emilie yelled that she wasn't mad. Hersilie, who had apparently been warned that a plot was being hatched against her, chose to follow the Baron of Kinkelin obediently 'so as not to give credibility to accusations of madness'.[1] She had only the vaguest of recollections of being committed to Charenton because she had been feeling so disturbed. Only endless paths, and the sound of doors closing, stuck in her mind; the only clear memories she had were those of her arrival into the convalescent ward: 'an enclosed space . . . clean and calm'.[2] The next day she learnt that Baron Kinkelin was none other than Dr Pelletan, her half-brother's doctor, and that she had been committed for spiritism and religious monomania with hallucinations.

Apart from these brief testimonies we are left to imagine what the first impressions of the asylum must have been. Ordinary hospitals were frightening enough; they were not places where people were cured, but the pathetic antechambers of death. Remember Mademoiselle de Vandreuil's persistent refusals to have Germinie Lacerteux sent to hospital. Hospitals evoked not only the fear of dying in poverty, but also of what would happen after death: in Eugène Suë's *Mystères de Paris*, Fleur de Marie and her companions were terrified as they imagined their own bodies handed over to scalpel-wielding doctors eager to practise dissection.

If this was the attitude towards hospitals, what could it have been towards asylums! They were hospitals, but 'special' hospitals. This made them all the more frightening, and gave these places and their inhabitants an aura of mystery. They repelled and attracted simultaneously. Like all disreputable places, asylums encouraged fantasies, sadistic and masochistic desires which in turn gave birth to myths about asylums. It was said that the air there was unbreathable, poisoned by the fumes emitted by diseased minds, and that these fumes were the agents of contagion. People were rumoured to go into asylums sane and come out mad, and the suicides of alienists who lost their minds trying to make the mad sane again seemed to confirm the stories about asylums.

These theories of contagion were taken very seriously if an 1841 petition by the people of the town of Autun is anything to go by. The townspeople protested against the establishment of a special hospital in their town; they feared 'the mephitic atmosphere created by a crowd of unhealthy people'. Moreover, they feared, the asylum would disfigure the countryside where the people of Autun took their Sunday walks. The town council was not surprised by the arguments of the people who signed the petition (often under false names). The council complained about the selfishness of these protests by reminding people that asylums were 'a method of relieving the sufferings of humanity',[3] rather than by denying the truth of the allegations which had been made.

Asylums fired the imagination and tales of illegal committal were common. Jules Vallès remembered them when he visited Sainte-Anne. 'One hardly dares cross the threshold, remembering the tragic stories told by those who had managed to escape. There are rumours that perfectly sane people came here and were locked in cells as if they were mad. You can count those who escaped but not those who stayed behind.'

From the asylums would come the screams of these 'heaps of human rags . . . shaken . . . by the terrible wind of madness'.[4] Rail travellers were terrorized by the cries of distress, like the screams of people being skinned alive, which came from the walls of Sainte-Madeleine which they had to pass on the way from the station to Bourg-en-Bresse.[5] The inhabitants of the town complained of the madwomen's screams, of the insults which they directed at passers-by and of the fact that they sometimes even threw stones at them.

What did newly-committed women remember of these myths and visions of horror? Even if we assume that their illness made them forget the nightmarish reputation of asylums, the architecture was terrifying enough. Patients were likely to have known and to recognize the huge walls, the gate and the chapel of the Salpêtrière. If they came from the town where the hospital was, it would have been impossible not to know the imposing mass of asylum buildings. Asylums were always present, even when they were on the outskirts of towns, on waste land which had been claimed by wanderers. They might have been built on the banks of a river prone to flooding as at Leymes, but they were more often on high ground. The choice of the site was important; by putting asylums outside towns, society showed that it rejected madness, and the distance involved protected the rest of the inhabitants from the alleged violence of the mentally ill and from contagion. But by building asylums on high ground, they became visible; although they were outside society, they cast a threatening shadow over it!

The threat could be even stronger if the madwomen were seeing these imposing buildings for the first time. This was not rare. The asylum-centred therapy of the time was based on a substantial network of special hospitals. The terms of the law of 1838 were clear: 'Each department must have a public institution especially for taking in the insane and looking after them, or it must come to an arrangement to this purpose with another public or private institution in the same department or in another department' (Article 1).

We are a long way from the dreams of the alienists. From 1838 to 1860, about twenty asylums were set up. The department of the Seine was particularly behind, while the numbers of mentally ill people had increased considerably because of the joint effects of immigration, living conditions and of the attitude towards the mentally ill which was more repressive than therapeutic. On 20 March 1860, a report by Girard de Cailleux estimated that there were 24,213 Parisian women in asylums. The facilities provided had not changed since 1801 and the Salpêtrière, Charenton and private hospitals could not contain the flood of female madness. It was necessary to resort to contracts with provincial asylums, which took in patients who had already been committed into asylums in Paris.

But even there the network of asylums was inadequate. At the end of the century, thirty-six departments did not have a public institution. Often the existing asylums were not able to meet the demand of the catchment area. In these circumstances, women were lucky compared to their male counterparts. The men were the ones who were sent far away for treatment, beyond the boundaries of their department. The madmen of the Pas-de-Calais were treated at Armentières and at Lommelet, but the madwomen stayed in the Pas-de-Calais at Saint-Venant.

The provision of asylums throughout France was uneven, being based both on demography and the existing infrastructure. Despite the weakness of the department of the Seine, the north-east had the best provision. Asylums were set up at the furthermost boundaries of each department, in uninhabited and uncultivated areas. This geographic distribution made asylums into an unknown world or another planet for the woman patient who would usually have travelled very little.

These factors must all have made the patient's first encounter with the asylum even more difficult. We can easily imagine the effect which the drawbridge and the gates between two towers at Bonneval would have had on a mind which was already disturbed. All asylums were not like medieval castles (which still evoked ancient fears of the power of the lord of the manor), but many of them were far worse. The limited means available and the urgency with which asylums were needed meant that non-medical buildings were often converted into asylums. The institutions were frequently in the premises of old prisons. At Saint-Joseph, madwomen were put up in the same premises as 'the penitent ex-prisoners and the convicts of Marseilles'.[6] There is a clear analogy to be drawn between asylums and hospitals and indeed it was a truism for the madwomen.

In fact, a large number of them were genuinely confused since they had been taken there by the police and most had gone through the 'depot' at the police headquarters. Reports of the time attacked the 'depot' as unworthy of families and individuals and complained in particular about the resemblance between the stay in the 'depot' and 'detention within the walls of a prison, which is always ambiguous and painful'.[7] It was a waste of time and effort. Despite the fact that when the hospital of Sainte-Anne was opened, a central office was set up, the 'depot' continued to exist.

The fact that as from 1872 it had a new name the 'Special Infirmary for the Police Headquarters' made no difference to the institution or to the harm it did. Hersilie believed that she was 'accused' of spiritism!

The ambiguity was reinforced by arriving in an asylum; not only were inmates shut in, with the full complement of locks and keys which that involves, but they were also depersonalized. When they were committed, women had to leave behind all their personal belongings and put on an inmate's uniform in the same way that prisoners would put on convict's clothes. Having to wear this uniform was 'a dreadful persecution' for Hersilie Rouy. 'The nuns began by taking away my little dog and sent her to the Countess R . . . The next day the warder on duty seized my papers and the 1,102 francs which were in my small Algerian wallet.'[8]

These actions were necessary to make the new patient into one of the inmates . . . her fellows. Hersilie did indeed join them and was lost among them for fourteen years.

A refuge from modern civilization

Keeping guard over the mad, and safeguarding society – the pun is so easy to make that we readily forget that asylums had a therapeutic purpose. More than that, they were in themselves a form of therapy. Locking people up to treat them, and treating them by locking them up were two indissoluble principles for the founders of psychiatry. Locking up the patient meant withdrawing her from the context which had caused the disturbances in the first place – clashes with families but also the nefarious influences of modern society, which the alienists condemned.

The society which they attacked was not Judeo-Christian civilization, but the newly born world of the Revolution and of revolutions. Their accusations were subtle: they were not aimed at the new ways of living but at those people who were judged to be badly adjusted to them. The 'special doctors' considered that civilization had positive aspects for the bourgeoisie they repres-ented. But they believed that using this new civilization well required an intelligent approach which was beyond the abilities of the poor man. Social disorder was the consequence and was used as a scapegoat to explain madness. Social changes become factors which caused disease. The alienists used major political upheavals, the accelerating rate of progress, decaying moral standards, the move away from traditional religious belief and the fluctuations of industry and commerce to support this point. Doctors also bewailed the decline of Christianity which destabilized many people and weakened belief in authority.

As always, the working classes came out as the scapegoats. Their lack of balance was accentuated by the exodus from the countryside and the industrial revolution. The loss of nature in the Rousseauist sense of the word was seen as partly responsible for the damage inflicted on this generation of mutants. It was alleged that under the influence of 'boundless ambition' some migrants from the countryside 'faced with their needs, deprived of the protection and support of the traditional guilds felt too weak to put up a fight; discouragement and poverty led them to lose their minds.'[9] This kind of analysis, more religious than scientific in tone, did not lead to a political analysis of pauperization. The inability of individuals to survive poverty was attacked rather than the existence of poverty itself. Civilization crushed the weak, but as Doctor Parchappe stated, 'The fall of a few cannot hold back progress for the greater number. Society should not slow down, but only has the duty to give greater and more comprehensive help to the losers of the great battle of life, fallen as victims in the wars of conquest . . . '[10]

RECEPTION PROVISIONS IN ASYLUMS

Society offered an asylum to these victims – it was the Asylum. Medical terminology was clear – hospitals were safe places where the insane were to be protected. The alienists wanted etymology and reality to coincide. Pinel dreamed of an Eden offering peace to tormented lunatics, he dreamed of 'gardens of flowers full of beautifully decorated groves'.[11] In fact, madwomen had to shelter under the galleries of the Salpêtrière with the wind and rain beating in their faces as they shivered with the cold. The air, said the liberator of the mad, should be fresh and invigorating, the air of the banks of the Nile. In reality, as visitors approached asylums their stomachs were turned by the foetid and nauseating smells that came from them. The sanitary installations were faulty and faecal matter was decaying under the pavilions.

Fodéré wanted hospices to be built in sacred forests, magical solitary places, havens of peace within the upheavals of civilization. The truth was that a few flowerbeds could not hide the damp throughout the Salpêtrière buildings; the plaster was peeling off the walls; wood flaked off the doors of the cells, even the newest ones, like paint from the prow of an old drifting ship. Alienists would have liked to be the sovereigns of an Edenic domain, but they were in fact the sovereigns of a world where, due to lack of means, the limited resources which were available had to be managed carefully so that at least people survived.

The inspectors constantly criticized the material poverty of the asylums; they were all aware that it was not only a question of shortcomings in accommodation. The fact that the infrastructure was inadequate distorted the intended functions of asylums; they were not refuges where the mentally ill could lay down their burdens of mental suffering and relearn how to live within the safety of a sheltered environment. To the sufferings of insanity they added those of material destitution; the daily life of the insane consisted of mental and material misery. As the years passed this state of affairs was accepted as the norm.

In this context we can understand the number of books on the reforms needed in the organization of the special hospitals. These brochures, which all had fairly similar titles ('Special hospitals – what they are and what they should be'; 'On the organization of lunatic asylums') did not question the function of asylums but only the ways in which they functioned. Justified criticisms never brought about the closure of an asylum. The authorities would bewail, regret, advise and make suggestions but would never take decisions, because even a dreadful institution was seen as better than no asylum at all.

The inspectors' descriptions drew up a clear hierarchy of asylums and the present-day reader cannot help comparing their remarks with those of tourist guides. There were good and bad asylums; some deserved four stars and some were little more than brothels. Some were even worth a detour! Local brochures encouraged strangers to the area to visit the asylum at Cadillac or Toulouse, these 'magnificent institutions' which were opened by Dr Marchant in the 1870s.

The hierarchy of asylums was based on three criteria; space, hygiene and facilities available. In mixed asylums which were housed in pre-existing buildings, the women's quarters were in the smallest rooms. This was based on learned calculations: women are smaller than men, therefore they need less space; the capacity of their lungs is smaller, therefore they need less oxygen than men's lungs. It was in good faith, therefore, that the authorities gave to female lunatics the smallest share of an infrastructure which was inadequate for all its inhabitants. The difference was a few square metres of space and fewer windows, since all the provisions were inadequate.

Until 1852 the mixed asylum of Antiquailles-Lyon remained in a state which alienists thought long gone. The stairs were narrow, the dormitories were crowded, the dining halls were dark. The asylum of Dôle was also short of space and this affected the medical staff as well. The medical director had problems with accommodation, the bursar had one room and the housemen a cubbyhole! In Rouen, the madwomen lived in a monastic environment: the 800 women there in 1862 were piled into tiny rooms with flaking walls. At Marseilles the inmates of both sexes had to endure unbearable conditions. Until 1850 the asylum of Saint-Joseph retained the signs of its previous function as a prison; there was a shortage of space and light throughout. The inhabitants of the asylum of Saint-Lazare in Marseilles lived in even worse conditions. Two narrow courtyards (one for each sex) were supposed to be sufficient for 150 people to take exercise. Worse than this, in the 1840s there were no dining halls and food was distributed in the courtyards. The inmates had to eat standing up or crouching on the ground, exposed to the rain, the wind and most of all to the sun.

Dining halls were always the first to go when there was a lack of space in asylums. At the Salpêtrière, in the Trélat wards, all meals were eaten in dreadful conditions because of shortage of space until 1844. All the patients ate alone out of wooden containers which, even according to the doctors, stank. By asking repeatedly for a dining hall similar to the one at Bicêtre, Dr Trélat obtained to begin with four tables of ten places each to try out the idea. In 1844, he had thirteen tables. The 130 incurable patients were therefore able to eat at a table either from pewter bowls or from earthenware bowls, if they were able to take care of them. Whereas before this they had only eaten cold food, now they were able to have hot meals, and they ate much more. The results were positive both for the patients and for the asylum administration: 'This means that the patients are in better health, are happier and there are considerable savings for the management. The defects in the premises are the only reason why the number of tables cannot be increased.'[12]

Getting rid of the wooden bowls became a wager. Using earthenware bowls and forks, spoons and even knives with blunt blades was seen as a victory against illness, the expression of self-control. For the alienists this progress in sociability was proof of the positive effects of the moral treatment they advocated, but it was also the symbol of a different approach to madness. In the new dining halls of the Salpêtrière, there were no wooden bowls. On the tables with oilcloth tablecloths the following was set out for each woman: earthenware crockery, enough tin cutlery for a place setting and a glass.

In asylum conditions cleanliness was no mean feat. Hygiene became a focus for complaints, requests for reform and attempted improvements. The unhealthy aspects of asylum life were often directly related to lack of space; the density of the asylum population, some of whom were incontinent, made the air unbreathable. At Dôle the public rooms were not even ventilated. But there were even worse features. The lack of adequate toilet facilities or even the absence of any facilities whatsoever announced the presence of asylums before entering them. Again at Dôle and at Rodez, the toilets were foul. Dr Véron who was head of Rodez in 1858 called it a 'real death trap'.[13] The reforms he introduced led to only minor improvements. At Rouen asylum there were still commodes, at Saint-Dizier there were no toilet facilities at all in the cells. At Lyons the refuse was emptied into a hole in the stone of each cell and these were emptied through a duct in the walls. The whole area was surrounded by putrid smells.

The cells were like the blind in the kingdom of one-eyed men, the last remnants of punishment-based asylums. At Grenoble the doctor in charge decided not to use them until larger rooms were built in 1862, but few doctors adopted this sensible attitude. At Dôle the cells were mobile crates, at Saint-Dizier they were caves hewn in the rock, at Marseilles they were freezing and had no light; underground huts like dog kennels were kept for so-called 'difficult' patients – in solitary confinement, lying on rotting bedding, they were to 'learn' how to struggle against madness . . . and fleas. Aubanel had the rooms for raving patients destroyed. They had been three metres underground and water oozed into them as into prison cells in the past.

In this way we can see the gap between theory and practice. The classifications of illness were purely medical and philosophical categories; many special hospitals were not in a position to put into practice the recommendations to separate patients according to their illnesses. At Lyons epileptics were kept in the same room as those who were only unruly, both for men and women. At Braqueville, the asylum of Toulouse, manic and senile patients shared the same dormitories. More often than actually being mixed together in this way, women with very different types of illnesses were put in close proximity to each other. Inspectors felt it was intolerable that the areas in which convalescents and manic patients were kept should be close to each other. They wanted the cells to be as distant as possible from the centre of asylums, to avoid the screams being heard by the less sick patients. This draws a nightmarish picture, but it is important to remember that the acute cases are the ones which captured the imagination of visitors and made them forget the more positive aspects of the institution, or the satisfactory conditions in other hospitals. Sadly, our sources record criticisms more than praise.

The hierarchy between asylums meant that there was an acknowledged inequality between patients. Madwomen were not able to choose which asylum took them in. Their geographical position and their place of birth determined the catchment area of the hospital into which they would go. But above all it was wealth that counted. Far from toning down the differences between classes, mental illness emphasized them. The advertisements for private mental homes promised discretion, medical care and plenty of distractions for the patients. They boasted of the shady grounds, the health-giving air, the clean premises and sometimes, but not often, they boasted about their modern hydrotherapy facilities. Dr Guiand's nursing home was set up in 1804 by the generous gift of a man whose maniac son had been cured by the doctor. In 1821 it moved to a place called 'Le Roucas blanc':

> The view is beautiful, the air is clear and the grounds vast, surrounded by arid rocks. The vegetation is vigorous but needs better upkeep. There is plenty of water at the Guiand nursing home, since the slopes of the estate are planned in such a way that all the rain water can be used by the hospital.[14]

This is completely different from the town of thirty-one hectares that the Salpêtrière had become. It was an old, well-maintained family house. There was no overcrowding, and Dr Guiand junior looked after about fifty people there. At the time of the visit of the inspector of asylums from the Bouches-du-Rhône region in 1843, there were twenty female and thirty male residents. But the inspector felt that the nursing home was nothing more than a good boarding house because there was a lack of therapeutic facilities, particularly no showers, and Dr Guiand apparently had little moral influence and was 'cruelly ridiculed' by his patients. This, together with the fact that the administrative requirements of the law of 1838 were not respected, meant that 'a complete reform was necessary to turn it into a good mental home'.[15]

The mental home of Vanves followed the principles of Esquirol and Pinel more closely. It was founded in 1822 in a huge property near the forest of Meudon and Fleury, opposite the old Château de Condé. The site had clear advantages: it was healthy, quiet and picturesque, yet very close to Paris. The patients were housed in several buildings. The main buildings were built next to the original house. This made it possible to separate out the inmates and have more specialized premises, and also made it possible to keep a closer watch over the inmates while still giving them the illusion of privacy and freedom. Each section had its own living room, which suggests the sociable atmosphere, and the inmates were invited to dine at the director's table as often as possible.

As for the enclosed twenty-four acres of grounds, they received lavish praise in contemporary descriptions. The land was undulating, streams ran through the meadows and willows and poplars were planted on their banks. In another part of the garden there was an orchard, and elsewhere there was a flower garden. Walks and work in the gardens were the daily distractions of the ailing but wealthy bourgeoisie.

In public institutions differences in wealth replicated class differences. As a national institution, Charenton took in patients of both sexes divided into various categories. In 1852, twenty-six women belonged in the first category (1,425 francs), fifty-six in the second category (1,125 francs) and three in the third (828 francs). Different food was served to members of these different categories. For an additional 900 francs a year, patients could also have private maids. They could also pay for the upkeep of their wardrobe, and treat themselves to coffee and cocoa.

Within each category, patients were divided according to their pathology. In 1849, 124 women were categorized as calm, fifteen needed constant care in the infirmary, thirty-three of them were manic and had to be kept separate, forty-eight were senile and four were epileptic. The patients were assigned to specific sections: one was reserved for manic and senile patients, another harboured a mixed population of the semi-manic, of senile women and of patients under treatment. The last division was for calm patients under treatment or convalescing.

These constructions, called 'the castle', were approved of by inspector Parchappe who saw them as expressing the progress of the art of building asylums. On the other hand, the buildings of Notre-Dame, Sainte-Thérèse and Sainte-Geneviève were only good to be knocked down, since they did not even have washbasins. The patients had to collect in their hands the water flowing from the central fountains in the recreational areas. However, the overall picture was satisfactory. Small details like the fact that the windows had curtains, that there were cloakrooms, coat-hangers, twenty-four bathtubs and sulphur baths proved that the institution was basically healthy. These advantages were only to be found in the quarters of the madwomen, according to Parchappe, who underlined the differences between the ways in which men and women were treated. According to him women had everything and men had nothing.

But it was rare for women to have this relative material comfort. The fact that madwomen were sent to the asylums closest to where they lived also had its disadvantages. These tended to be the oldest buildings which were not purpose-built as asylums. Impoverished Parisian madwomen who could not afford Charenton had to join the other patients of the Salpêtrière. This hospital has already been described. It held some surprises for Hersilie. As an officially committed pauper, she was soon transferred to this headquarters of female incarceration. The patients were divided into five sections which were subdivided into groups defined by Girard de Cailleux in 1863. The first section contained only calm and semi-calm lunatics – including convalescents – senile or with minor illnesses. However, quite often manic patients were also included and this was criticized by Girard de Cailleux. Workshops and a reasonable canteen were available for the patients of the first section. There were not enough cells available, only one for every forty madwomen. The same subdivision existed in the second section, where the dangerous mix of manic and semi-manic patients was even worse.

The Mitivié section had twelve cells, one for every fourteen madwomen. With about 196 inmates in 1863, it was felt that this section needed to be radically reorganized. The common room and the dormitories with twenty-four beds were too small. The 150-place canteen was not well managed. There was a lack of basic amenities – for example there were no curtains in the bathroom. The problems of accommodation also affected security. The supervisors were too far away.

The third section was even more disturbing. Senile women, epileptics and idiots were housed in a building which was in ruins. The accommodation facilities were inadequate and the workshop could only take 150 women. The facilities were terrible, from the 250-place canteen, to the two ridiculous bathrooms or the disgusting toilets. The doctor's consulting room faced the same problems.

The fourth section was no better. The calm and partly calm patients were packed into unhealthy dormitories in an airless attic where it was too hot or too cold. Senile and paralysed women were gathered on the third floor, and because of the lack of space the other patients wandered around in the corridors. There were twenty-five cells in this section. Neither the sick bay for those suffering from physical illnesses nor the garden made up for the other problems.

The fifth section included a sick bay and a dormitory. It had a population of about 290. There were thirty-nine cells. Girard de Cailleux felt that this was inadequate given the number of manic patients. There were far too many of them, which meant that they were mixed in with calm and partly calm madwomen. The admissions facilities were in this section, already firmly inside the asylum. This was seen as unfortunate because it helped blur the already faint boundaries between nervous strain and real madness. Those who were least ill suffered from being housed with patients who had very different illnesses. And new patients could stay up to a week in the admissions ward before being sent to their section. Throughout the hospital, but particularly in the corridors, there was not enough air because of the overcrowding. This reached such a peak in the epileptics' wards that the inmates from those wards were redistributed throughout the hospital.

If patients suffering from different illnesses were mixed together, so were patients from different social classes. The latter was a threat to moral standards. Prostitutes were found alongside other women. Girard de Cailleux spoke of 'an attack on the dignity of poor but honourable families where it is suffering that has led to madness. For the former, madness is almost certainly the consequence of a debauched and immoral life.'[16]

Each of these sections was an asylum in itself with its own doctor. The patient would remain there unless the alienist advised otherwise or the patient made a request. Changes were made with the agreement of the management. This was headed by a director, backed up by a bursar and eleven clerks. The sections were numbered but also given a title. Hersilie was passed on from the section for frenetic patients at Rambuteau (the Trélat section), from the Grandes Loges (Mitivié wards) to the Chalets. The section for manic patients was called the Chalets because fourteen small chalets were used as isolation cells for the raving patients. This area was isolated from the rest of the hospital by a high wall.

This area was clearly overcrowded and, as a result, unhealthy, and this is even after the improvements of 1863. After 1820, 209 unhealthy cells had been demolished and the recreation areas enlarged. Corridors had been built and were used for different purposes, as refuges, workrooms and even canteens. Stoves were installed; before they were put in, the patients in the cells had to put up with the cold and some of them would die of hypothermia. The heat circulated through openwork doors which also made it easier to keep an eye on patients. The locks blended into the panelling and therefore didn't stand out like the old bolts which had been reminiscent of prisons. Similarly, ordinary windows had replaced the narrow slits of the former cells and the upright bars had been replaced by cast-iron frames divided up into squares, making double windows which were not filled in with glass.

Unfortunately, by 1852 the interiors of only twenty-five of the cells had been renovated: the furniture consisted of an iron bed, a chair and a bedside table. To fight the cold and damp, oak floors had replaced stone slabs, but there were still 101 cells where these changes had not been made. As for the chalets of the 'Swiss village' built in 1836, in 1852 they still had no heating.

Because it proved impossible to transform the infrastructure of the Salpêtrière radically, the hospital turned to the provinces for help. Its population was reduced by transferring patients to provincial asylums. The first records of this practice date from 1839, and the numbers increased greatly as time went on. In 1844, the first large-scale transfer took place, involving 400 patients from the Seine region, including 200 from the Salpêtrière.

However, facilities in the provinces were also limited. In his statement on the budget for the financial year of 1850,[17] Dr Morel of the Maréville asylum demanded an immediate improvement in the standards of living within the asylum. He had just arrived at the hospital and had attempted to end the indiscriminate herding of patients. He wanted to set up categories which were based solely on type of illness and excluded any social criterion. He put forward a three point plan for housing female patients: the senile women who were housed alongside the fee-paying patients would be moved, the old oilworks which was unhealthy would be knocked down, and an area would be built for manic and epileptic patients. These alterations were all the more necessary given that this institution, built to house 600 patients, in fact housed 785 patients of both sexes at that time. And Maréville was by no means an exception!

In 1861 Girard de Cailleux, in the *Annales médico-psychologiques,* denounced the practices in short-stay asylums. They were much too small; the capacity of the dormitories and canteens was only seven cubic metres instead of the twenty-four required in many cases. It was impossible to find land which had not already been built on. The patients were not divided up into categories and epileptic, manic and semi-calm patients were often mixed up. The hygiene conditions were dreadful. Under the pressure of numbers, the administration of asylums failed to comply with the requirements of the law of 1838. The records were not properly kept. Incorrect information was often taken down when patients were admitted and this led to legal problems. Hersilie Rouy became Joséphine Chevalier. She left the Orléans asylum under this name, with the additional details that both her parents were unknown. J Manier also told the sad story of a Miss Antonia Monasterio who could not be found by the police. She had disappeared into the labyrinths of the asylums, probably after being registered in the wrong name.[18]

THE MODEL ASYLUM OF AUXERRE AND ITS LIMITATIONS

While Hersilie no doubt suffered like many women who were moved between the asylums of Fains, Maréville or Orléans, in her travels she also experienced the opposite extreme. This was Girard's asylum at Auxerre. This hospital, which became a psychiatric institution in 1840, was entrusted to him by Ferrus who wanted him to create a model asylum. Girard's original plan and the many reports he wrote on the subject reveal his insatiable desire to make the patients more and more comfortable. He wondered how many bathrooms were necessary, how much space each patient required and also considered other measures, decorative as much as therapeutic. For him, the two were not far apart.

The works which began in 1846 were given a strong boost in 1849 by Haussmann's intervention. They yielded results. Girard made the best out of the site, which was a chalky piece of land at the foot of the small Saint Simeon mountain; to the east, the asylum faced the banks of the Yonne, to the west the Mont Saint Georges. To the north there were fields and to the south the hospital was surrounded by a circle of trees through which one could see the towers of the cathedral. The women's section was crescent shaped. The administrative buildings and the men's section were away from the main courtyards.

The hospital buildings were specialized. The women's section consisted of three pavilions of living quarters. Each contained three dormitories with gas lighting, one on the ground floor, and the other two on the first floor. The patients were divided into four categories: senile and demented idiots, maniac epileptics, raving maniacs and calm maniacs who were convalescent. Visitors were in raptures at the proportions of the dormitories and their cleanliness. There were 350 cubic metres of healthy, breathable air for sixteen patients, who slept in polished metal beds. A gleaming parquet floor was kept clean by the staff with the help of the patients. At the head of each bed there was a shelf, and each inmate could hang up her clothes, labelled with her patient number. She could also put her toiletries on the shelf.

The supervisor slept in a room next to the dormitory, and could keep an eye on the patients from her bed. The rooms of the resident doctors were next door to the rooms of the convalescents, who were already outside the troubled world of madness, but still subject to medical attention. To fight against the tendency to become bedridden or bored and the attendant risks of chronic illness, each area contained a canteen, a meeting room and a courtyard with covered galleries full of plane trees and decorated by fountains which Girard loved.

Four smaller buildings were joined on to the main pavilions. They were either therapeutic (baths, workshops and cells) or functional (laundries, wood stores, stables, sheds, tanks). Research had gone into designing the cells so that the cries of the raving patients could not be heard. Girard chose a ray-like plan which dispersed the patients' screams. Some attempt was also made to improve their daily life: next to each cell there was a small yard where the patient could walk 'freely', sheltered from curious onlookers. They could enjoy nature, something which the doctors believed to have soothing properties. A small opening in each door made it possible to combine isolation, freedom and observation. One of the innovations of the asylum at Auxerre was a concern to reconcile these seemingly opposing ideas. The great number of ditches or ha-ha's meant that the inmates could look out beyond the asylum while still enclosed within it.

Hersilie responded to this sense of space and freedom. When she arrived in 1863, rather than being critical as usual, she noted in her diary: 'Everything is gleaming, pretty, and well ventilated; there are galleries with pillars everywhere. You can see that Haussmann has been busy. There are no walls in the gardens but ditches hidden by rose bushes which make it possible to see out to a distant horizon.'[19]

She was given a small room for three people where a female warden also slept. For once, she agreed with the authorities. The inspectors boasted about the quality of staff and wardens and how easy it was to supervise the patients. They praised the fact that life was regulated but not monotonous; there were no bars or locks, so reminiscent of prisons. The success of Auxerre made Girard famous, and led to the name 'de Cailleux' being bestowed on him, as well as a host of compliments including one from a member of the regional council. During a visit to the hospital, he addressed the director in the words of Molière: 'I can only congratulate this gentleman for ending up in your hands and tell him that it is lucky to be mad to enjoy the effective and pleasant cures which you so graciously offer.'[20]

Yet, there were still problems. The accommodation for fee-paying patients was too close to the medical wards and the wards for the violently disturbed patients. Despite their ingenious construction, the cells were also too near by, and therefore noisy. On the other hand,the director's house was too far from the heart of the hospital and he wasn't aware of everything that was going on. These small details didn't tarnish the hospital's reputation, but stopped it from being an entirely perfect model for other establishments despite the wishes of the inspectors. Whom should we believe? The administrative visitors who were easily satisfied, or Hersilie's reports? She claimed that 'Haussmannization' did not affect the whole of the hospital and that the wards for senile women and the cells remain unchanged. This was too much to be just a coincidence. She claimed that in 1862 they were still dreadful, and bore no relation to Berthier's description of the same date.

They are square, a little longer than the wooden bed that they contain. A commode is next to the bed. That is all the furniture. Both the bed and the chair are attached to the wall. There is a courtyard of the same span as the cell and twice as long for each cell. It is surrounded by high walls so that the recluse can see absolutely nothing and nor can anyone hear her. She can only hear the cries of indescribable suffering of her unfortunate neigh-bours. Nothing could be more awful. Two of these cells are such that the woman can be tied on to the bed and on to the chair and the room can be made completely dark. That kind of treatment can make the sweetest and most gentle person into a raving lunatic . . . it can make people want to kill themselves.[21]

Apart from these differences of opinion, there was general agreement. Everything had to be renovated and reorganized. The Salpêtrière, and its male equivalent Bicêtre, seemed to have incurable problems which, according to contemporary accounts, embarrassed the capital. To do something about this dreadful situation, the post of General Inspector of asylums was set up in 1860 and, of course, given to Girard de Cailleux. Investigations led to plans for a central asylum in Paris, and for satellite asylums outside the city. There were also plans for an admissions office to end the scandalous 'depot', and for special asylums for epileptics and idiots.

So the authorities finally admitted that even during the golden age of the asylum there were serious problems. The decrees of 1863 ordered that the asylums of Sainte-Anne, Vaucluse and Ville-Evrard should be built. The opening of Sainte-Anne on 1 May 1867 was not enough to stop the anti-asylum campaigns which were putting an end to the golden age of asylums and of alienist medicine.

THE PROBLEMS OF RUNNING THE ASYLUMS

All asylums were inadequately funded and this influenced the way they were run. The lack of money affected those who managed the hospitals. Measures adopted because of economic problems were presented as having a therapeutic basis. For example, uniforms were intended to make all patients seem equal, to level differences in social class and to create the character of the inmate. But this only applied to paupers. Fee-paying patients were allowed to keep their own clothes. At Saint-Yon they even had to keep their own clothes, and new ones were provided by the families.

As far as women were concerned, uniforms were seen as part of the cure; they were necessary to treat cases of ambitious monomania which focused on beauty, and they were also part of the struggle against 'excessive vanity'; some madwomen liked to adorn themselves with ribbons, to wear eccentric clothes which made passers-by notice them. For these women uniforms were a way of not standing out and keeping uniforms clean became a measure of how integrated into society they were.

This was the official line, which didn't even always fool the doctors themselves. They underlined how sad patients were when they had to give up their own clothes, their only links with their past lives, and a proof of their identity. Hersilie somehow managed to hold on to a dressing gown and a shawl. As she moved from asylum to asylum, holding on to them became a daily battle, the way of not being assimilated to the mass of lunatic paupers.

Doctors used this attachment to clothes. Even a new white petticoat was a reward and being given a whole outfit for a visit or a party was wonderful! This game was complex and illogical. Why unlearn interest in your appearance and happily wear the uniform so that you can be rewarded by being allowed to pay attention to your appearance for a few moments?

It was difficult to be vain in a uniform. They were drab, sad and reminiscent of prison. In theory, the inmates should have a summer and a winter wardrobe. At the hospice of Cadillac in 1840 in the Gironde, the winter wardrobe had twelve components: one headscarf or headdress, one dress kerchief, one dress in homespun material, one apron in woollen drugget, one red felt skirt, two twill pockets, a knitted waistcoat, one pair of woollen stockings, a coat, a pair of wooden clogs and slippers, and two shirts for weekday wear. In summer the wardrobe for women consisted of a blue dress, one cotton skirt, one neck kerchief, one pocket handkerchief, one headscarf or headdress, one pair of cotton stockings, one pair of shoes, one headscarf to wear at night, and two twill pockets.

Even this limited 'wardrobe' was scarce. The inmates in Paris only had one set of clothes for all seasons, because the resources given by the department, the commune, the hospices fund and the families were inadequate. The 11.50 francs which were allocated per inmate at the Salpêtrière in 1841 meant that the patients were 'inadequately dressed' in thick, grey woollen cloth, which was much too hot in summer. From 1842 the funds were increased and this meant that clogs could be replaced by shoes. Clogs were impractical and sometimes dangerous since they could be used by violent patients as missiles and had wounded many people. 'English' leather shoes were hardly more costly than ordinary shoes and stopped patients from taking off their shoes. They were tied to the feet by a strap held on by a screw tightened by a little key which the nurses kept. These shoes were alleged to cut down on chest complaints because the patients could no longer walk barefoot on cold tiles or damp soil.

The asylums near the Seine didn't have the right wardrobe either. In 1842, the inmates of Maréville suffered from the climate because they didn't have any eiderdowns. And even if the wardrobe given to patients when they came into the hospital was adequate, the fact that many patients were violent and not able to control their bodily functions meant that clothes rapidly deteriorated. Then came the insoluble problem of how to replace the inmates' wardrobe – totally or partly.

One of the crucial aspects of asylum life and a constant worry for the director was underwear. The lack of both linen maids and linen made cleanliness very difficult. This was not such a problem in women's asylums or mixed asylums where the female inmates were put to use. Washing all underwear – an operation sometimes called the great bacchante – disturbed the usual lethargy of asylum life. It created complex organizational problems; there was a hierarchy of washerwomen based on the degree of mental illness. The least handicapped patients would beat the clothes against the washboards and make sure that they were clean; the more feeble-minded would spread the clothes out to dry. There had to be enough staff to keep discipline, and avoid disturbances. But many asylums didn't even have a laundry. In 1850 a laundry was set up from scratch at Maréville so that patients could have more than one complete set of underwear[22] and they could give their clothes in to be washed.

At the Salpêtrière the shortage of staff and equipment got worse with time. The rate at which clothes were washed and changed is disturbing: one group of patients only got clean underwear once a month; as for the sheets, when it was rainy they were only changed once every six weeks because they took so long to dry. Things improved towards 1850; although laundry rooms were still not well enough equipped to reach the required level of cleanliness, they were good enough to provide a service. The chief of police of the Seine then decreed that surplus cloth from spinning mills should be given to the hospitals. To reduce the drying time, the Salpêtrière was given a washer and dryer which could deal with 4,000 kg of underwear or 600 garments in sixteen hours.

But these improvements didn't reach the provinces. Dr Icard, who had run the Cadillac Hospital since 1867, was still complaining in 1875 about the 'near total shortage' of underwear and clothes.[23] The staff was unable to improve the situation; the patients wore torn clothes and the doctors realized the effect this lack of hygiene had on some patients. It was almost impossible to keep the senile patients clean. Even their underwear was taken away, with no respect for modesty, usually so important. The frenzied patients had to exchange their ordinary clothes for canvas straitjackets, made out of a rough material which didn't follow the shape of the body and made it difficult to move.

The second obsession and despair of the staff in charge of cleanliness was bedding. It should have been changed regularly but the shortage of mattresses, covers and sheets was such that this was not possible. At the hospital of Cadillac each madwoman was provided with a metal bed, a straw mattress, a woollen mattress, a feather bolster, one pair of sheets, two woollen blankets and a quilted counterpane.

To try to solve the problem of bedding for senile women, mattresses were replaced by sheaves of straw. This practice was common but given that the bedding was very rarely changed, it offended both hygiene and comfort. Their quarters were a breeding ground for illness. At Auxerre, an even more radical solution had been adopted; it shocked Hersilie:

> In the other institutions I have seen, at least the senile patients had a straw mattress. When the straw is wet, it is changed; there are warm bedclothes and, generally, the straw is only under the seat; the head, back, hips and feet are on a real mattress cut into pieces. At Auxerre, for paying patients nothing, nothing, nothing. Patients are on iron beds. There is webbing on it and a basin underneath, a blanket which cannot be tucked in because there is no strap; as a result it moves about as the unfortunate creature on the bed shivers night and day on this kind of hammock. I have only seen this at Auxerre. It is horrifying. If savings of this sort on straw, sheets and time are made for paying patients, it must be even worse, if that is possible, for paupers.[24]

But some hospitals were very ingenious; the most inventive ideas concerned beds, used as a lavatory by incontinent bedridden patients. Hersilie does not mention the ingenuity of the infirmary at Auxerre: there were polished metal beds fixed to the floor. Twenty centimetres above the bed was a heavy cloth hammock; in the centre was a big zinc plate open in the middle; the hole took urine into a zinc vessel fixed to the floor by an apparatus to which only the supervisor had the key.

More frequently, there were 'container beds' or box beds. A locked drawer was used a a lavatory. At Riom the nuns had imposed strict discipline which was more effective than these various devices. Incontinent patients were put to bed at seven o'clock in the evening; the nuns woke them up at ten at night and at four in the morning; the patients followed this monastic practice without complaining and the cleanliness of these wards was legendary.

The second constant preoccupation of the bursar's office was feeding the asylum. Budgetary constraints had to be reconciled with the need for a healthy diet, which the alienist doctors saw as part of the overall treatment. In 1877 Girard de Cailleux underlined this again when he pointed out that doctors hadn't forgotten the truth of the saying 'sanguis moderator nervorum', and did their best to make patients eat well. They had to be given a balanced diet which would stimulate constitutions affected by illness and keep away scurvy and atonic illnesses to which the inmates were prone.

There was a limited choice of foods; some were not appropriate for the patients who could easily choke or those who refused to eat. Menus were drawn up with great care and the three daily meals were planned in advance. Medical prescriptions might alter parts of the meal. Here again the asylum left nothing to chance. The annual menu was fixed to the nearest ounce, and was part of the hospital's regulations. For example, at the hospital of Cadillac breakfast consisted of soup, milk, chocolate or coffee on demand, and 312.5 grams of bread. When the doctor prescribed it, patients might receive in addition, say, 18 cl of wine, 31.2 grams of cheese or jam, or a piece of fresh fruit. Patients were not likely to go hungry after lunch or dinner. Lunch and dinner both included 321.5 grams of bread and 18 cl of wine. On top of this, lunch consisted of 50 cl of soup, 187.5 grams of salad, or the same amount of green vegetables, and 125 grams of boiled meat off the bone. The meat could be replaced with 92.75 grams of cod, 125 grams of fish, one and a half herrings, 187.5 grams of meat stew or 250 grams of fresh vegetables. For dinner, patients also had 187.5 grams of meat stew, or depending on the day the same weight of green vegetables, or 93.75 grams of rice, 250 grams of fresh vegetables, 2 eggs or their equivalent in milk products or fresh fruit.[25]

Budgetary limitations increased the gap between paupers and paying patients. The times of meals and their contents varied according to social class. Patients were grouped according to three criteria: gender, status and illness. At Saint-Yon the type and amount of food given to patients depended not on medical prescriptions, but on which of four categories the patient belonged to. The fourth, or lowest class still had jam for dinner, but the paupers had none. Unexpectedly, both paupers and paying patients were given alcoholic drinks. At the asylum of the Bon-Sauveur at Caen, the daily ration for women was one litre of cider in 1856 and one and a half litres for men. The ration could be increased to three litres if the patients worked. The cider was quite strong.[26] So alcohol was provided by the asylums for the patients. Drunkenness, not drinking, was frowned upon. In 1857 an official prescription regulated this. At Sainte Anne, the amount of wine given to women was 12 cl a day, as against 16 cl for men. By 1870 only two or three asylums did not conform to this general rule.

The reports of the inspectors were far from being as optimistic as Cadillac's plans. They criticized the lack of meat in the diet and the excess of green or fresh vegetables. They also criticized the fact that meat was often replaced by processed pork meats. This imbalance resulted in stomach problems. The inspectors paid more attention to quantity than to quality. It was very rare that they should condemn poor cooking as they did at Marseilles. Hersilie complained of the daily menu at Orléans, which was made all the more unbearable by the lack of hygiene in the kitchens.

> As soon as clean water arrived, instead of emptying the glasses and the bowls into a special bucket before rinsing them, Julie threw all the scraps into the clean water saying that it made them nicer for the pigs. The cloths used to dry these dirty bowls were then put out on benches and chairs where incontinent patients would go and sit. It is quite understandable then that we had to overcome our feelings of disgust before eating, and we found it very hard to find anything but dirty scraps to eat. Soup was served with pieces of bread handled by women who left them lying around on the table after having gnawed them and broken them up with their filthy hands. Miss L and myself used to take away as much as possible to throw it over the wall or into the latrines so we could eat a bit less reluctantly. One day she called me and showed me the servants' kitchen. They used to eat clean food and washed their dishes separately. She showed me Marianne with both arms uncovered who was stirring our lettuce with her bare hands in a can where she had just added a drop of vinegar and water as a dressing. It was all we were having to eat, but we couldn't face it and were reduced to dry bread only.[27]

The partial – in both senses of the word – nature of this information makes it impossible to draw a conclusion.

Very few inspectors exposed the trafficking in food: the 'legal trafficking' of the leftovers of the paying patients' meals, or the illegal trafficking which linked together the paying patients, paupers and staff – poverty could be exchanged, bought and sold with empty promises. Tobacco bought at the asylum shop was a strong currency and could be exchanged for fruit brought in by visitors; but parcels from families were exceptional. It is impossible to evaluate the exact food resourses in asylums because of seasonal variation and the differences between asylums. To overcome their inadequate financial resources, the administrators tried to make asylums self-sufficient. Self-sufficiency was itself made into a part of the treatment. The success rate varied depending on the land available, the climate, the fertility of the soil and the ability of the inmates to do the work. In all-women asylums there were always difficulties in getting the heavy manual work done. Women mainly helped in weeding the gardens, picking produce and carrying food.

One fact remains. The infrastructure of asylums could be and always was improved by the power of money. Seen from the outside, money was so little in evidence in the paupers' part of the asylum that it made no major differences except to a few. But given the moral, physical and material poverty which inmates faced it is likely that these small things meant a lot to them.

The rhythm of life

WORK

Idleness was not tolerated in asylums. It was seen as synonymous with chaos. It was seen as inimical to mental balance; unstructured time was the breach through which reverie, fantasy and frenzy might penetrate the asylum. The excessive numbers of patients provided yet another excuse for organizing daily life to a strict rhythm. The day was divided into periods which were not structured around the doctor's visit but around work. Once again this shows the ambivalence of the way in which the 'organs of the asylum' functioned. Work was presented as therapy, and although doctors were certainly aware that it was econcomically necessary for patients to work, they were silent about its primary importance to material survival and instead extolled its therapeutic benefits. The regulations of Sainte-Anne's hospital had no compunction in stating that 'work is instituted as a method of treatment and provides a distraction for the patients' (point 9, section XVII).

If ever a therapy was social, this one was: paying patients who refused to work were not forced to, in private establishments work therapy did not fool families, who argued that they were paying for treatment and turned it down. So, to prevent the inmates from sinking into total idleness, distractions had to be found for them, rather than work. Thus at the asylum of Lafond at Cognehord near La Rochelle, the fee-paying patients spent their time sewing, doing embroidery and knitting; they made tapestries, artificial flowers, looked after their clothes or played music.

The vocabulary used by the contemporary writer reflects the distinction which decorum required him to make between paupers and fee-paying patients. The former were 'women', the latter 'ladies'.[28] As wealthy families did not agree to manual work, the management of the asylum of Sainte-Méen in Rennes planned in 1860 to set up a billiard room and a gymnasium in the part of the asylum for paying patients. Gymnastics had already been introduced at the asylum of Saint-Vincent-de-Paul in the Rhône area.

The destitute lunatic, on the other hand, had no right to be heard and neither did her family. The entry for 'lunatic' in the Dechambre dictionary states that incurable lunatics, 'the majority of productive workers', were one of the elements vital to the prosperity of asylums. These paupers woke up early. Asylums began to get up at five or six in the morning depending on the season. This was not easy. The first step was to clear up the mess of the night. Nurses were backed up in this thankless task by able-bodied patients. This was followed by prayers. The required reverence was often difficult to achieve and, depending on the piety of the nurses, required more or less work. The calmest patients, unless they suffered from religious monomania or demonomania, were allowed to go to mass. The presence of the chapel made asylums look like villages. Although chapels were sometimes hidden, they usually stood out clearly and acted as the symbol of the presence of God, that ultimate presence among these outcasts abandoned by the rest of humanity, by all sane human beings.

But the medical profession was not agreed on the benefits of religious practice. Even when it was under control, religion remained a source of potential disturbance for the imagination of patients. Religious concepts, it was said, generated wrong ideas, and distanced the lunatics even further from the physical world to which it was the task of asylums to return them. Others saw religion as the source of peace, of moral solace. The degree of respect shown for the chapel was seen as a valuable guide to the patient's state of mind, and doctors quoted with some astonishment many examples of restless, unruly patients who would briefly become peaceful and well-behaved for the blessing. Religious feeling was seen as one of the last bastions to fall to the onslaught of madness.

Once this brief moment of peace was over, the working day began. There were only minor differences between asylums. The first part of the day was short because at about seven thirty it stopped for the doctor's visit; work then started again until around nine or ten when lunch was served. A break allowed time for relaxation, then the lunatics went back to work until four in the afternoon. Dinner and another break came before the last part of the day, which finished at around eight o'clock and often later, particularly in summer. The day was rounded off by a last prayer. Only severe illness exempted lunatics from working. Work required a certain level of lucidity, cleanliness and physical fitness, therefore those who were incoherent, senile or paralysed were excluded as well as all those who were bedridden. This amounted to approximately one patient in four or five in Paris around 1860 (no distinction is made in these figures between men and women). The proportion of working inmates therefore depended to a large extent on the catchment area of each asylum. The percentage of able-bodied patients affected the amount of work allocated to each individual.

Asylums tried to make use of even their most handicapped patients. The feeble-minded could sweep up, and those who were even more unfit spent their days shredding linen for bandages. But in the final analysis the patients' activities depended on the infrastructure of each institution. Where possible, agricultural and industrial tasks were associated. But hospitals which were attached to a farm and had enough workshops were few and far between. In rural areas the problem was partly compensated by allowing patients out of the asylum. But this kind of measure could only apply to the peaceful patients and of course had to be supervised by hospital staff. At Pontorson asylum, women took part in harvesting hay, wheat and fruit in the surrounding countryside. In 1847 the director complained that this solution was not satisfactory and did not make big savings for his institution.[29]

Some hospitals had no workshops at all. At the asylum of Saint Lazare in Marseilles this meant that no work at all was available. Until 1844 the Trélat section at the Salpêtrière, which had 434 beds (not including beds for nurses), was so crowded that a workshop could not be set up. Sixty-four patients were linen workers and worked in the dormitory itself. The great transfer of 1844 which, as we have seen, affected 200 patients at the

Salpêtrière eased the overcrowding in the section and made it possible to set up a workshop at the same time as a canteen. But the other side to the coin to the improved facilities was increased demand and twenty-eight days after its opening the workshop was overcrowded with 109 linen workers. The canteen had to accommodate those who made bandages, but also around twenty seamstresses, and once again lunatics with different illnesses were put together, although this practice was frequently exposed as a harmful one. In 1842 the Trélat section numbered 104 working women out of 460 patients, and in 1844 the proportion was 316 workers out of 374 patients.

There was not much variety in their work, which was typical women's work – the kind which is never noticed, although it is essential. As one would expect, linen and laundry take up most of the available labour. It was not surprising that in 1851 Dr Parchappe should see building a laundry as one of the most important things to do when setting up an asylum: 'In such a vast institution the amount of work involved in a laundry provides a precious source of work for women. It is important to make the best of this in asylums for the benefit of patients or for the profitability of the institution.'[30] In 1842 there were 68 women linen workers, and 129 in 1844. From this point on they tended to take up sewing in the new workshop. Each had her own job title, as in a factory. The maids, the visiting room attendants, the shoemakers, the women who made braces, those who carried saucepans around, the household servants, all worked busily but never frantically because the supervising staff kept time, called to order the 'sleeping and the dreaming', orchestrated the rhythmical movements of the hands of the 143 women who made dressings. The asylums were like hives, like a swarm of well-disciplined worker bees. No wonder that alienists tended to overdo animal and vegetable imagery in relation to asylums!

Sewing and linen were the main occupations everywhere, though sometimes a greater range of activities was on offer. At the asylum of Blois, a mixed institution of seventy-five patients with thirteen women patients, all the women were involved in the entire process of manufacturing clothes and linen, from spinning the thread to the finished product. Apart from this demanding job, they had to act as kitchen maids and do the washing and ironing. Workshops were also set up for the inmates to make other objects, not specifically described apart from wooden shoes. As for the men, they were agricultural workers and bricklayers or stonemasons.[31] All these tasks were carried out under the supervision of the staff, though they sometimes resorted to using the healthiest patients to back them up, creating a hierarchy among the patients. The county asylum of the Gers had two workshops, one for sewing and one for spinning. They were run by two women who were 'unpaid workers', and were themselves supervised by sisters from the Order of St Mary. The workshops had to be quiet and peaceful, and any lunatic who disturbed the peace was turned out immediately.

Improvements in the infrastructure of asylums produced an increase in the number of female inmates working in the Paris asylums. In 1856 Bicêtre and the Salpêtrière reached about the same percentage – 68 per cent of men and 69 per cent of women worked. The mentally ill ran the farm of Sainte-Anne. They ran a pig farm, a cowshed where shoes, straw hats and doormats were also made. During 1852 about 900 women workers at the Salpêtrière made 6,569 drawsheets, 5,836 stockings, 878 overalls, 922 caps, 1,429 nightshirts, 29,307 shirts, 18,715 sheets, 2,285 neckerchiefs, 1,595 dresses, 1,251 towels, 1,153 aprons and other small items which were not described in detail. To this textile production must be added the manufacture of 90,274 non-specified objects.[32]

The lunatics therefore made a substantial contribution to the running of the asylums and this rapidly became essential. They were paid for their work. The linen workers of the Trélat section were paid wages which varied from 261.20 francs to 544.70 francs between January and September 1844.[33] The salary actually paid to them varied according to the hospital's budget, since they only had to be paid for work done for the outside world. The salary was calculated every year and its aim was to benefit only those who worked. Part was kept by the Assistance Publique and used to cover staff costs and the costs of making workshops available for patients. Article 15 of the hospital regulations of 18 December 1839 specified that a third of the product of the lunatics' work should be given to them and two-thirds of it retained by the administration.

This was applied inconsistently. Some inspectors even stated that because paupers benefited from public charity it was economically as well as morally illogical to pay them any money. The heads of the hospitals had no compunction in backing up these purely economic arguments with the declarations of successive Ministers of the Interior who periodically issued reminders about the true function of work in asylums. Since it was seen as a subsidiary method of treatment its primarily economic function was hidden. In this way it was easy to hide the very real economic exploitation of lunatics behind the screen of therapy. Life in the asylum was a life in which the mentally ill were exploited.[34]

TIME OFF

The peaceful regularity of life in the asylum rapidly became monotonous. Any minor irregularity became a major event. The relentless rhythm of life was broken by two events, outings and parties. Some patients dreamed about these outings into a world in which they were now strangers and which was therefore strange, but others who were completely institutionalized were disturbed at the thought. As they climbed into the carriages taking them out of the asylum, they were very worried.

Outings were complex for all involved, including the staff who accompanied patients. Although this favour was only granted to peaceful patients, and they were rarely in groups of more than five, patients might suddenly break out or behave very peculiarly. The carriage was fitted with various coercive devices, and straitjackets were ready in case they were required. The carriage would be carefully protected from curious onlookers as well as from the patients themselves, and would then leave the town for the countryside, and of course the much vaunted peace of nature. These escapes were only available to a tiny proportion of patients despite the fact that staff accompanied them. In some institutions they were only for fee-paying patients. This apparently discriminatory measure was due to a lack of staff. At Rouen only patients in the top category were allowed outings, and they had a special supervisor. Since some patients had escaped, non-feepaying patients were deprived of this breath of fresh air.

Parties and fairs in particular were the main way of breaking the monotony of life in the asylum. They became a tradition in special hospitals during the nineteenth century, but were never really accepted. Critics were many and had three main complaints: they didn't like the fact that fairs were open to the public; that the inmates' work was on display; and they objected to the festivities themselves, tombolas, dancing and fancy dress, seen as the worst possible therapeutic aberration; sane people would adopt imaginary personalities, play with fantasy, mingle with the insane disguised as countesses, bakers, caucasian princes, or wearing other extraordinary outfits. They made wonderful fictional characters, and it was impossible to forget that they themselves were deliberately mixing reality and fantasy. Although the carnival atmosphere and fancy dress in particular did take patients' attention away from their illness, it also meant that fantasized alter egos were encouraged to rise to the surface and that this could reactivate madness.

Maxime du Camp remembered seeing madwomen looking dazed at these balls. He also encountered epileptics 'with their skins stretched across their unhealthy and swollen faces', and 'an old hunchback dressed as a lunatic; she was clearly a nymphomaniac and walked around two or three men who were there, holding out her thin arms to them with a hungry expression on her face.'[35] The lunatics made a spectacle of their madness, parodying it in their costume and blurring the barriers between the worlds of sanity and insanity. A caricature of a symbol: at the end of the century the hat of the alienist doctor Legrand du Saulle, dead in 1886, was always present at these fairs!

The possibility of rubbing shoulders temporarily with the insane gave fantasy a free rein and explained the attraction which the lunatics' balls held for those outside the asylums. The ball of the Salpêtrière, known by the public as the madwomen's ball, was one of the curiosities of Parisian life. It is difficult to assess how much the success of this ball was due to voyeurism and how much to the feeling of intoxication which contact with the insane seemed to provoke. Doctor Fredet was one of the guests at the Salpêtrière ball in 1889. As a detached observer, he was surprised by the agitation which took over 'men and women who had come there to see a new spectacle';[36] he noted with amusement that their noisy excitement made it easy to confuse them with the inhabitants!

Usually, both guests and inmates were similarly restrained and this was praised. At Lannemezan the asylum was opened to the families on the day when there was a fancy dress parade. The journalist from the *Nouvelle République des Pyrénées* who covered the event on 8 August 1851 emphasized 'how difficult it was to tell which of those in the crowd, among the various groups of people, had been struck down by a mysterious illness and which were the luckier ones who were able to carry on the struggle of daily life.' Experiences like this were grist to the mill of those who defended balls. These people said that those who believed (or pretended to believe) that all the madwomen in the hospital were allowed to be at the ball were being naive. Many women were excluded: patients suffering from frenzy, nervousness, erotomania, nymphomania, and those which Fredet called 'major' and 'minor' hysterics. He described these hysterics as 'the human wreckage of an overly stimulated and sensual life, of desertion and poverty'.[37] The advocates of these balls pointed to the long-standing quality of their organization and the presence of doctors ready to intervene if required.

The balls took place in a long, brightly lit room, decorated with flowers and plants. In the early years an inmate played the piano; her cacophony was later silenced and replaced by a large professional orchestra on a podium in the middle of the hall. At one end there was a buffet covered with delicacies, a special treat. Two benches along the walls were provided for those who were thought too mad to take part. Sometimes they would be entertained by a conjuror, under the watchful eyes of the supervisors. The dancers were young. They danced up and down in pairs without any over-excitement.

This calm behaviour was used by the people who supported balls to strengthen their case that balls could be therapeutic. They claimed that the physical exercise involved was soothing in itself and the peculiarly feminine pleasure that balls provided was good for patients. Music was believed to have an important influence as it relaxed the nerves and soothed melancholia. But the effect of balls extended beyond one night. For two months before the event it gave inmates a cheerful topic of conversation. Workshops were livelier because the inmates had to decide on their costumes and make them. Balls gave a purpose in life and an aim to the endless succession of days and repeated actions which made up asylum life. That in itself was a victory over madness.

It was easy for staff to make this important event into a reward, a carrot which was promised for good behaviour, and discipline was much better in the period before the festivities. Fredet nicknamed them 'The ball of the incoherents': incoherent the patients might be, but they had not lost their taste for the pleasures they used to enjoy and had kept the same hierarchy of values. This was the one chance in the year they were given to prove that they were able to adapt themselves to a new situation.

Outings and balls acted as lifebuoys which only few inmates could hold on to to break up the monotonous rhythm of hospital life and to escape temporarily from the asylum. The others who were deprived of this had recreational rather than intellectual activities to improve life. Singing, of religious music in particular, was introduced into all asylums and became well established in many, as at the Salpêtrière and at Saint-Yon where lessons were given by a teacher. The inmates were also able to enjoy sessions of reading aloud while they worked; the books varied from religious texts to moral tales, history, geography, travel books and poetry and plays. Patients were sometimes allowed to take away books for private reading if the institution had a library. But these distractions also had a therapeutic element and were orchestrated by the doctors. Patients were denied freedom of choice.

In theory, visits were a more straightforward escape from the world of the asylum. The doctors would decide when patients were ready to make the first contact with the outside world of sanity. For short periods, asylums were no longer cut-off, isolated little worlds. On Thursdays and Sundays, from twelve to four o'clock, the entrance to the Salpêtrière was crowded and up to 5,000 people went through. Despite their limited means, voluntarily committed patients apparently benefited most from the privilege of having visits. The structural changes in 1845 meant that most committals were official ones, and doctors noticed that the number of visits decreased. This is further proof that the family life of officially committed women had collapsed. This left them in emotional isolation and was one of the main reasons for their madness.

Obviously the geographical isolation of the provincial asylums exacerbated the loneliness of the patients. Visits were often cancelled because of the time they took and their expense. Patients from the department of the Seine transferred to provincial asylums suffered in this way. Visiting rights varied between asylums, depending on the attitude of individual doctors. At Saint-Yon, Parchappe only gave visiting rights to patients who had nearly recovered, and to inmates who were calm but incurable. The hospital was open to the people of Rouen on Thursdays and to people outside Rouen on the other days, except Sundays. This did not make visiting any easier. To compensate for this lack of communication between patients and their families, Parchappe sent the families monthly health reports.

There were very few interruptions, then, to the monotony of 'life' in the asylum. The daily timetable shows just how little time was available for medical treatment. Asylums guarded their patients rather than treating them.

5

TREATMENT IN THE ASYLUM

All doctors needed to be able to diagnose and prescribe appropriate treatments. This was always on the basis of their professional knowledge, of course, but it was also informed by their preconceptions about women. One basic prejudice (a scientific truth to alienist doctors) stood out – more women than men were mad. Pinel thought that women's nature made this so. Esquirol considered it to be socially based. This shift from a biological to a social explanation may seem to represent a move away from *a priori* judgements. In fact a theory, shaken by statistical evidence, was in the process of being restored. By involving itself in questions of 'relative liability to madness', the fledgling science of psychiatry was effectively moving into the realm of the unverifiable. Parchappe often attacked the old saying that women were predisposed to madness. Girard de Cailleux demonstrated that the association of madness and committal was misleading – more women than men were committed. Apart from these two clearly defined positions, the debate generally returned to questions of 'more mad' or 'less mad'. And it all had one common feature: the indictment of female nature.

Isolation: a method of speeding up treatment

After Esquirol, the therapeutic benefits of isolation were accepted. Isolation was intended to modify the perverse set of mind and affectations of the insane. It was seen as the most vigorous and usually the most effective way of fighting mental illness. Committal was therefore in itself a therapeutic action. Treatment in asylums was recommended for men and women equally. They offered a variety of different kinds of confinement. There was straightforward committal with the right to receive visitors after a few days' observation by staff and doctors; there was also a stronger version in which all contact with the outside world was forbidden; and finally there was total isolation in solitary confinement.

Carefully screened visitors were allowed more often in asylums for men than in all female institutions, where any signs of sexual deviance meant that all visits from men were systematically forbidden. Committing prostitutes – those symptoms of social gangrene – meant taking them away from their diseased milieu. Confinement also stopped erotomaniacs, nymphomaniacs and hysterical women from having any contact with men who might fire their desires, and provoke attacks. Only husbands and very close relatives were exempt. Visits, usually monthly, were closely watched by the alienists, who used them as tests. The patient's state of mind was measured by the calm and affection she showed her visitors. The special doctors held that women were calm and affectionate by nature, and had a strong sense of family. If a patient complained about being committed, or was indifferent or violent towards her visitors, it meant that she had made no progress, and that she should indeed be kept apart from the others.

Confinement could also be a protective measure. Lunatics whose property was not in the care of the courts were often victims of fraud. Relatives and friends were often guilty here, but so were strangers to both hospital and patient, who would come in when plays were being performed. This scandal was denounced in the newspapers, and fraud stopped only when new regulations controlling access to asylums were introduced. The general administrative council of hospitals, civil hospices and home care in Paris ruled on 2 November 1842 that no one was to enter any part of an asylum occupied by patients without the express authorization of the director of the institution concerned.

Patients were also allowed to sustain their links with the world outside by letter; they could write one letter every two weeks, and sometimes every week. Under the law, the institution had to give inmates the freedom to write letters, and this meant providing them with the materials with which to do so. In practice this was frequently not the case. Doctors felt that letter writing was the kind of activity which could revive patients' obsessions and focus their attention on their illness. This was seen as a particular risk for women, who were generally held to have innately vivid and morbid imaginations. Hersilie Rouy had to trick the management in order to send off her letters of complaint. She used friends she had made in the asylum, whom she called her 'devoted inter-mediaries'. She also had to hide in order to write her memoirs.

Throughout her internment, she constantly wanted to write. Unfortunately for us today, these accounts were destroyed by the asylum management and they even took away pencil and paper from her. To succeed in bearing witness of what was happening to her, Hersilie managed to hide a few scraps of paper in a handkerchief. These few sheets of paper are in themselves symbolic of her suffering. Hersilie said she wrote them with her own blood.

Therapeutic arguments against letter writing were often a mask for a medical and administrative fear of attracting inspectors, who could appear as a result of letters which escaped to the outside world. In addition, it was not unknown for letters to be returned to the hospital by the authorities. If we believe Hersilie, Dr Renaud de Motey, acting head of the women's department of the Maréville asylum, gave the order in November 1860 that 'all letters should be sent out except those which contain complaints about the hospital.'[1] Hersilie also told a story of a fee-paying patient who was beaten by her maid and told her husband about it in a letter. Apparently, her mail was torn up seven times. Incoming mail was also censored. Dr Foville complained about the alleged lack of discretion of the medical staff who went so far as to read patients' letters. The number of complaints from patients' families suggest that this accusation was justified.

Communal asylum life was supposed to promote reintegration into society. This was dependent on the patient's ability to relate well to other inmates and staff. Any violence, even verbal, indicated failure and the patient would be put into solitary confinement – excluded from this already excluded world. Confinement was classic asylum practice, even at Auxerre. Parchappe regretted it, but admitted that it was impossible to give up temporary confinement. Renaudin wanted to abolish it and replace it with the use of straitjackets. In their jackets, patients would be tied to their beds. Which was worse? The straitjacket was no improvement on the boredom and monotony of solitary confinement. It also caused cramps, poor circulation and skin problems. It was clearly less shocking than punishing patients by locking them up naked on beds of straw.

Very few hospitals abolished confinement. Those which did (like Maréville in 1854) were only given a few lines in the *Annales médico-psychologiques*. Instead, authorities tried to limit its use, or treat patients more gently. In 1843 the inspector for the Bouches-du-Rhône region boasted that solitary confinement as it had been used existed no longer.

> If the inmates were at all excited, they would have been locked up night and day in a cell. The problem would be solved by locking them in. The only attention they received was to be given new bedding, and food, through a narrow window with iron bars. Today, we only resort to this severe regime very rarely, and for very short periods of time. As soon as patients are calmer, they go back to living with the other inmates.

The inspector's honesty, however, led him to tone down his praises.

> This is what the doctors prescribe. I have to say that their instructions are not always closely followed. On 8 January I found about twenty cells on the ground floor containing patients who could quite safely have been free.[2]

The inspector had the cells opened. He freed an unfortunate young woman from Aubagne who was totally stupefied. Locked up in her cell, she spent her time buried in the straw with only her head showing. She had been living like this (the inspector wondered if living was the right word) for some years. When she was allowed out of the cell, she walked around the courtyard without causing any trouble. Out of the twenty women freed, only Clementine proved intransigent. She had to be put back in her cell because she tried to take the tiles off the floor of her room on the first night. This was only a temporary measure, though, until a special room with a beaten earth floor was built for her.

The fact of being a woman – with a fragile constitution which needed protection – did not stop women from being put into solitary confinement. In the minds of the doctors the criteria which applied outside the asylum did not apply to madwomen. It was as though madness had hidden their femininity. Any violence women showed had to be repressed by violence, if they were to regain their femininity. Aggression in women was less dangerous than male aggression, and could be repressed by a whole arsenal of coercive methods, ranging from ropes to straitjackets. These devices didn't remove patients from asylum life altogether, but did distance them somewhat by preventing the expression of subversive words and gestures. Patients were terrified of solitary confinement – a sword of Damocles hanging over them. It was pure horror, as those who had survived it made quite clear. It was a hell where women wailed, whined, barked and screamed. Correction and cure were inextricably linked in asylums. They formed an integral part of moral treatment.

Moral treatment or re-education

If the insane were to be cured, the founders of psychiatry believed that patients first of all had to accept that their own way of thinking was wrong, or that the fears they had were unjustified. Their disturbances could then be cured through moral treatment, by being listened to and treated gently in soothing isolation, far from the world of violence.

This basically philanthropic moral treatment was not suited to asylums. The overcrowded world of the asylum needed a structure; there were too many patients, too few doctors who were too rarely present. Despite repeated requests from the administrators, doctors didn't always live in the hospitals. All this made it impossible for moral treatment to be used as originally conceived. The treatment was rapidly debased and reduced. This explains the therapy which was actually used by the special doctors. In their writings alienists stressed the importance of non-physical causes of insanity. Georget was the champion of this line of thinking. In his view, 95 per cent of cases of madness were moral in origin. The male constitution protected men from the vicissitudes of the emotions; women had no such protection and were easy prey to madness. Georget brooked no disagreement, and shrugged off statistical evidence against his theory. According to him all these proofs were worthless, because women were great liars. These lies, he maintained, were a manifestation of what modesty they had left. They concealed the unspeakable 'need for union between the sexes, all the stronger because it was repressed, but encouraged by reading novels, or going to the theatre'.[3]

Alongside these bitter and unscientific diatribes, his philanthropic voice could be heard, lamenting in shaking tones the problems that many women faced: distance from their homes, lack of affection, lack of financial security and dependence on the whims of their husbands and employers. He could even shed tears over the fate of these 'women who let themselves follow their hearts to become the victims of cowardly seducers'.[4]

He attacked excessive interest in love. According to him, love affected respiration and circulation. Autopsies of madwomen who had died of passion showed lesions in their epigastric centre. For Esquirol this was proof that the seat of the emotions was not in the brain. Passion was essentially irrational; it was doubly so when compounded by an irrational choice of partner.

The case of Camille (who 'perverted' a younger man) has already been mentioned. It was not the only such case. These perversions – incest was the worst – worried the doctors, and led them to treat their patients very severely. The pathologizing of sexual deviancy stripped women of any responsibility for their own actions. It was all the more strange, then, that alienists should turn around and convict women – the very women whose responsibility in these actions had only just been denied.

Ulysse Trélat was the champion of these paradoxes. Adèle, eleven, was committed because she had perverted a young boy of fifteen. She was diagnosed as having such low intelligence that she could medically be labelled as an idiot. This did not stop Trélat, however, from claiming that women like Adèle were 'Bacchantes . . . who lacked the self-control or modesty without which women are not women. These creatures are too flawed to be able to benefit from their freedom.'[5]

It must be said that this kind of attack is rare in the surviving records. Trélat advised committal for life, and deplored the fact that not all other doctors agreed with him. The doctors of the Salpêtrière were more moderate and their choice of words less inflammatory. In Adèle's case they would also have assumed that she was incurable, but as long as her state was not dangerous to anyone else they would have been happy to release her. In fact, Adèle was released, although her subsequent fate was grist to Trélat's mill. She was returned to her mother (of whom we know nothing), became a 'camp follower' and an alcoholic. She became pregnant and died in childbirth.

As for homosexuality, it was so much against nature that it was not seen as depraved passion but as the result of a physical abnormality. Lesbians were called 'tribades'; they were not subjected to moral treatment, unlike sodomites. Since they did not have an atrophied penis, they were still human, and their vice was seen as mental rather than physical, in the classical tradition.

Alienist science had only one moral cure for female excess, whatever form it took. And the forms it took were varied: excess in matters cultural, excessive pride, ambition, or involvement in politics. The cure involved replacing the madwoman's own scale of values with a new one created by the doctors. They had to give up their passions, in order to become docile and hardworking. The infrastructure of the asylum existed so as to shape the lunatic. It made no difference whether or not the patients understood why their behaviour was unreasonable, provided that they stopped behaving in that way (or were seen to stop). Esquirol was prepared to enter into the illusory world of the insane in order to prove its vacuity, but the other alienists refused to play this game. They told the patients that their thoughts and behaviour were unreasonable, and demanded that they should stop. The patient did not need to untangle the mechanics of his or her illness with the doctor's help. Rather, it was for the patient to follow blindly the model behaviour proposed – or rather imposed – by the doctors.

Doctors now became the governors of these lost souls. Patients were treated as grown babies. They had 'gone wrong', and alienists were there to put them back on the right track. The consequences of this type of moral treatment are clear. Symptoms became disproportionately important. Patients were seen to respond well to therapy if they suppressed their madness and hid it from the doctors. But what was then considered a great improvement might now be seen as self-control and repression. This was the case with Miss E. P, a beautiful young seamstress committed to the Maréville asylum for ambitious monomania in March 1842. She believed that she was the fiancée of a nephew of Napoleon, heir to the French crown. She was convinced that there was a plot against the Orleanist dynasty, and that Louis-Philippe would be overthrown. She was convinced that she was being overthrown and preferred to die as a queen, so she slit her wrists and tried to drown herself. Her doctor, Dr Macario, decided to apply moral treatment, which he called, with honesty, intimidation. The explanation that her ideas were fantasies was given to Miss E. P under a cold shower. The doctor warned her that she would be given painful treatment which would end her illness. Macario described the treatment in the following terms:

Miss E. P's attention was focused on what was about to happen by the way in which the doctor was talking to her and the apparatus around her (she was put in a covered bath with the shower hanging above her head). She opened her eyes wide and looked surprised and anxious; she obviously feared a major disaster. The doctor made a sign and the fatal tap was opened; the water burst out and fell on Miss E. P's head. From the first jet of water, she screamed with fear and begged us to stop. She promised to give up all her delusions of grandeur. She told us repeatedly that she was only a poor young woman who had to work for a living. We read her story back to her point by point and emphasized each of her fantasies. She recanted everything she had said and assured us that she had been mad but was not mad any longer. The next day when Miss E. P was put into the bathtub, she told us how happy she was

to be free of her fantasies and thanked us for helping her. She said
that she would like to go back home and take up her work again.
She was only a poor working woman, just a worker and was not
going to marry the nephew of the emperor, nor was she going to be
queen of France. . . . On 16 March she still had some doubts and
had gone back to some of her fantasies during the day but in our
presence she controlled herself.[6]

The picture is totally clear. Being cured, or at least being better,
means silencing the fantasies. But if a patient didn't express her
fantasies because she was too frightened to do so, could she really
be said to be better? Fear became a therapeutic tool which was
used in all asylums although doctors did not always give it the
same weight. For some doctors it was the pivot of all treatment.
These were the followers of Leuret who asserted loud and strong
that 'moral revulsion' was the best method of treatment. According
to him, suffering – even physical pain – should not deter the
alienist doctor, he should act like 'hunger which pinches the
stomach' or 'a worrying courtcase'. Macario belonged to this
school. He believed that reasoning with patients was not effective
and that better results could be reached by being severe and
using punishments. In a word, his treatment was based on fear.

For other doctors, fear was the ultimate weapon. Ulysse Trélat's
stance on this point was full of subtle nuances. He wanted people
'to be kind to the lunatics', who were deprived 'of the most
important things in the world, truth and freedom'. But they
should be shown a special sort of kindness, not the sort which
applied to ordinary people. 'We want them to be ruled and not to
rule.' Trelat's care for his patients and his devotion to them became
a legend; but his care was only shown after his patients had been
committed. This was essential in his view in order to protect
families. Lunatics had to be branded in order to keep them from
making contacts with others, which would 'blight the most
intimate pleasures of the home and threaten the family's right to
have heirs worthy of its name'.[7]

Some, like Archambauld, were disturbed by the use of fear and
violence. He wondered what their therapeutic effects were, and
he was concerned that monomania might turn delirious under
their influence. These suspicions were shortlived but they did
gradually undermine the reputation of these types of shock
therapy. This was reflected in various ways – a few lines in the
Annales, the odd remark in medical records. It all served to sow
the seeds of doubt about this type of treatment.

As in the case of the use of cells, what was presented as therapy was often repression dignified by scientific language. If the patients did not follow the rules of the asylum (following timetables, keeping clean, working hard, taking medicines, keeping quiet, answering doctors' questions, respecting other patients and visitors), they were said to be argumentative, haughty, undisciplined and difficult to control. Consequently they needed to be treated or punished. Treatment or punishment? The two words were in practice so similar that doctors often used them interchangeably. The insane had to be punished for being abnormal, and treated to put them back on right path. Hydrotherapy was the cornerstone of this repressive treatment. The incomplete evidence from the Salpêtrière suggests that all newly committed women were given showers. Hersilie's day at Charenton began with a bath. Dr Calmeil thought this necessary because of the vivid imagination, not to mention persecution complex, of the new arrival. She was angry at being committed. The first bath lasted one hour. According to Hersilie, this was an average length. For once she shows some humour, saying that 'they obviously didn't think I was too mad, because the length of the bath corresponds to how mad they think you are.'[8] Six-hour baths were commonly prescribed, and they could sometimes be twice as long.

Showers consisted of jets of water aimed at the patient, through a pipe held by a member of staff or fixed to the ceiling. Depending on the diameter of the pipe, the experience was more or less violent. If the treatment went for too long, it could cause fainting or even death. Moreau de Tours had this therapy tried on himself several times and found it very hard, even though 'he had asked not to be treated too roughly.'[9]

Alienists disagreed in theory but in practice they all used fear and violence. At least those who openly advocated these methods were clear about what they were doing, and they were used as scapegoats by the second group, who claimed to oppose violence but used it secretly. Debate about the use of the 'no restraint' approach, which rejected all forms of physical constraint, was not as active in France as it was in England at the same period. Showers were given in covered bathtubs. The cover, or shield, went up to patients' necks and stopped them from moving. It was made of iron and often injured patients. At Sainte-Anne it was made of stiffened cloth. Moreau de Tours was struck by its similarity to the guillotine. Patients also made this link and were terrified. Some studies, like that by Rech, examined the effects of the shower, depending on the position of the patient and the temperature of the water. Most alienist doctors, however, asked themselves no questions, since the shower was first and foremost a repressive practice.

Guislain usually defined it as 'moral bloodletting', and an instrument of discipline. This pseudo-hydrotherapy became the keystone of treatment in the asylum. Doctors used and abused it. When Hersilie continued to complain, she was shackled by the collar into the bath on three separate occasions. There she was doused with about fifty pails of cold water. When the punishment was over, she found out why it had taken place. She had helped another of the inmates who had fainted, she had forgotten to return a pair of scissors to an overseer, and, finally, she had written a few words on a wall. Her story does not seem exaggerated. The few pieces of information scattered in hospital records confirm her account.

Other forms of hydrotherapy existed, both imaginative and sadistic. At Grenoble, the special hospital had a 'closed swimming pool' about six feet deep. The treatment involved the immersion of madwomen afflicted by melancholic stupor. Apparently this helped the patient to take exercise, restored the circulation, warmed the extremities and provoked an overall reaction. The bath was a tonic which re-energized patients. In order for it to be truly effective, it had to be preceded by a warning, so that the patient would be obedient, or would break her silence. It was therefore particularly suitable for apathetic and incontinent patients. The hospital at Auxerre had a 'confessional'. The name came from its shape. It was a little narrower than a church confessional so that the patient had to remain upright. According to Hersilie:

> The feet rested on a slatted floor, and water bucketed down in torrents from the top of the confessional. The treatment could last as long as the doctors wanted it to. It is apparently much worse than the showers because I have seen patients do the same things again after the shower, but never after the confessional.[10]

The word used to describe this kind of treatment covered both the shape of the apparatus and its function. It is true that madwomen had to confess their sins and recognize their faults, like children. The punishment for disobedience involved being treated like a child.

The way in which 'moral treatment' was applied could only reinforce the feelings of guilt and self-punishment so frequently a part of female madness. This can be seen in the case of Angélique,

Hersilie's companion at Orléans. According to the narrator, Angélique was 'pathologically disobedient'.[11] She was always hiding so that people would look for her, and would be severely punished for it. To stop her from repeating her 'crimes' she would be placed in a straitjacket, given showers or tied up. Hersilie even tells us that her friend was occasionally treated very badly. Once the staff apparently put her head in a bucket of water and tied her up so tightly that the skin of her arms was cut. When Hersilie found her tied up like this, Angélique had been guilty of speaking too loudly when she woke up and disturbing her companions. However violent the measures taken against her, she would never complain, but would laugh about it. As soon as she could she would repeat the same 'jokes' for which she had been given such severe 'medication' and for which she was taken to, and then detained in, the violent wards. Angélique's behaviour was the result of the therapy she received. The treatment had no effect on what she did. Hersilie tells us that Angélique would often put the ropes on herself. This proves that the 'moral treatment' was experienced by patients as a punishment and not as therapy. Angélique's lucidity about the motivations behind her treatment is deceptive. She was not lucid enough to rebel against this coercive violence, but made it part of her madness and saw it as necessary to her life. She did not perceive the lack of proportion between her actions and their consequences; she was unable to make the distinction and saw the punishment as reasonable. The 'naughty child' had been so well conditioned that she punished herself. Not capable of controlling herself, or motivated by masochistic desires, Angélique had her neuroses reinforced and not challenged by the therapy she received.

If the patients were to be turned back into responsible members of society, they had to work hard. We have already seen that work was part of the struggle against idleness, but it was also part of the process of rehabilitation. It focused the patients' attention on the concrete tasks of everyday life and dispelled their fantasies. Work, then, was the antidote to pride and ambition, and provided a form of social therapy which put every woman in her place. Working-class women returned to the work they had traditionally done – repetitive and poorly valued jobs like cleaning, washing and sewing.

The patients' progress was carefully observed and recorded. Case histories became school reports and merit awards ('Could do better', 'tries hard', 'lacks application', 'docile and does what she is told'). When 'moral treatment' through work did not have the effect the doctors wanted, repressive therapy would take over. The punishments for lack of application were not as severe as the shower. They resembled more closely punishments meted out to children – like not being allowed to have break times, tobacco or to go out on visits. There was a wide range of these punishments and different asylums had their own specialities. At the asylum of Saint-Joseph in Marseilles, patients who refused to take their medicine or broke the rules in any other way had to eat separately at a 'punishment table'.

The opposite also applied. Those who worked well were rewarded as a form of motivation. Rather than being given money (which it was feared might make them greedy), they were encouraged, given cakes, tobacco and presents purchased through private donations. A few people protested against the monopoly of manual work in asylums. Girard de Cailleux criticized the lack of variety of work, the fact that it was very tiring, and also the way in which the therapeutic benefits of working were being taken over by economic considerations. Applied in this way, work lost its moral virtues. Cailleux also saw a therapeutic function in recreation. At the Salpêtrière the patients could do gymnastic exercises. Doctors who advocated this hoped to concentrate the patient's attention on her body and thereby banish 'evil thoughts'. It was not a matter of a healthy mind in a healthy body. Most doctors compared gymnastics to work, in terms of how tiring each activity was. 'For the vast majority of lunatics', declared Lunier, Constans and Dumesnil in a report in 1874, 'outdoor work for men and work in the laundry for women is much better than physical exercise.'[12]

Distractions were also intended to attract the attention of the madwomen and turn it away from obsessions to more healthy matters. Singing had three benefits: music itself had a calming effect, and singing in a choir developed discipline and group spirit. If the institution could afford it, it bought a piano. Paying patients were often allowed to play it. At Stephansfeld, starting around 1845, they were allowed to go to evening gatherings. These entertainments were supervised by staff and their wives played an active part in organizing them.

Drama and reading, which we have already discussed, were therapeutic tools to be used with care. Like the lunatics' ball, plays could revive fantasies and were highly controversial. It was argued that they not only confused reality and fantasy, but also ran the risk of restimulating the ambition of women who would be applauded as actresses. As far as reading was concerned, anything which might stimulate the imagination or the emotions was censored. Alienist doctors were suspicious of literature and saw it as one of the predisposing causes of madness. They condemned romanticism totally, because it emphasized feelings of the emptiness of life and made its adherents into potential lypemanics. It also encouraged ambition and pride. For doctors, the statistical dominance of mental disorders among intellectuals was partly due to the success of romanticism among the cultivated classes.

These risks were much higher for women because their imaginations were more easily roused than men's. When someone leads a soft and inactive life the risks of this happening are all the more serious. This explains the contents of asylum libraries – religious and moralistic works, and descriptive travel literature. When the library at the new hospital of Sainte-Anne was opened, the following books were banned: *The Mysteries of Paris*, *The Wandering Jew* and the *Seven Deadly Sins*, by Eugène Suë; *Notre-Dame de Paris* and the *Orientales* by Victor Hugo, but also *Uncle Tom's Cabin*.

Educational activities were seen as far better. A few exceptional asylums had schools for the inmates. They were for a tiny minority of patients, those who were calm and could concentrate. At Stephansfeld, Dr Roederer only opened these classes to convalescents. This was all the more logical because in his view moral treatment was only relevant during convalescence. In practice, schools supplemented other activities. When there was no work in the fields they kept inmates from idleness. Developing education systematically was made very difficult for the staff, given the impossible task of teaching. In 1847, a M. Duffrene organized teaching at Stephansfeld and tried to teach patients to read. At the Salpêtrière a woman teacher taught lunatics the alphabet.

Here again the lack of contemporary reports makes it difficult for us to assess the impact of this very rudimentary teaching, which was as much a form of distraction as anything else. Teaching never went beyond this basic level. The state of the patients was not the only explanation for this. Alienist doctors were products of their own culture – they did not question the value of education but rather the ability of the patients to absorb and use it. If it were wrongly used, education could deprave them, pervert their intelligence, corrupt their morals and lead to moral degradation.

Learning was foreign to women's very nature. The growing

science of psychiatry took on board all the most outdated clichés. It was believed that women lost their physical charms when they became cultivated; that education with any goal other than the production of good and pious wives was dangerous. Women's ability to 'be knowledgeable' was denied. The *Shorter Dictionary of Medical Science* turned prejudice into fact when it asserted that 'in general, learned women have no real knowledge. They mix up and confuse everything . . . They cannot focus their attention for long on one thing, and therefore they cannot enjoy the deep and strong pleasures of intense thought. More than this, they are unable to have these feelings.'[13]

The alienists went further. In their view, the mere thought of studying made women unbalanced. This was more because of the despair they would feel when they realized that their goal was impossible than because of the actual process of studying. It was held that women went mad through frustrated ambition and only men had the dubious privilege of going mad through 'too much intellectual work'. When Ulysse Trélat applied these ideas to Hersilie's case, she was labelled a lucid madwoman, suffering from pride, and she had the privilege of featuring in his famous book.

> Miss C. R . . . who is forty, came on to my ward on 13 November 1854, from Charenton. She is totally lucid. Not only does she answer questions accurately but she speaks well and can hold long, interesting conversations on all subjects. She claims to be a musician, has composed pieces which have been published, and sold. She claims to be the sister of a reputed literary man, and to have many friends in literary, scientific and artistic circles, and also in elegant Parisian society. She mentions many very famous names . . . She has given concerts in France, but mainly abroad, in London, Vienna and Berlin, and in all the main towns of England and Germany. These established her reptuation and earned her strong and long-lasting friendships . . . The dates are chronologically consistent and events lead on from each other. Any question is immediately answered, and any objection can be explained satisfactorily. At first glance, Miss R is not mad; . . .
>
> But as we studied and observed her in greater depth, we realized rapidly that she is a monomaniac riddled with pride, who took on the name of 'Golden Star', and attributed to this name a supernatural influence on her destiny. Since she is experienced, she hides this very well, but all monomaniacs give themselves away sooner or later through their pride. We found a star printed underneath a piece of music published by Miss R, and the same star under her signature at the end of her letters. 'What does the star

mean?' After a moment's silence, the question was repeated. 'Don't you know who I am? Or are you pretending not to know? I am the Golden Star. And if you don't know it, I will soon teach you.'[14]

Trélat felt that by putting herself on the astral plane, she was also putting herself above the rest of humanity and surrounding herself in mystery. He himself, who had been a member of the Lodge of the 'Friends of Truth', and of the secret society 'Help Yourself and Heaven will Help You', saw this as a sign of lucid madness.

The admonitions which were part of the moral treatments constantly reminded patients of their status as women and of their true nature. Women were thus trapped into a particular social position and a fixed biological identity. The physical equivalent of the moral treatment involved the control of women's bodies and their treatment as part of the mental treatment.

Femininity: treated or mistreated?

MENSTRUATION AND THE RHYTHM OF MENTAL HEALTH

The normalization of femininity necessarily involved a healthy menstrual cycle. When a patient arrived at the asylum the doctors would observe her periods and take notes of the regularity, quantity and colour of the blood. Periods were supposed to act as a purifying agency which cleansed the body of harmful impurities. Nevertheless, menstruation was dangerous since it also created fertile breeding grounds for madness, or even caused it.

Brière de Boismont told the story of a woman who, when she was menstruating, 'discusses subjects which bear no relation to her usual interests. She discusses history, geography, politics and writes verse and polemics.'[15]

More often menstruation generated violent impulses which women could not resist. Well-brought-up women would become skilful thieves. The premenstrual days disposed women to suicide, personality disorders and apathy, and made them disgusted with life. One of Dr Belhomme's patients, suffering from suicidal monomania, decided to drown herself. Determined that her family should not get her body back, she decided to avoid Paris and went to Saint-Cloud, where she hoped that nothing would stop the current from dragging her body away. On the way, her period started. Her madness dramatically ceased; she was cured and went back home.

So the onset of menstruation could cure an illness which was only caused by the biological disturbances which preceded a period. In this theory periods were responsible both for the illness and for the cure. This is why doctors concluded that even if menstruation made women more fragile, it was normal and necessary. Restoring a regular menstrual cycle was one of the major aims of asylum therapy for women. To do this doctors used hydrotherapy. Warm hip baths were supposed to relieve the congestion in the body. Full baths also helped, and in general the temperature was between 30 and 35 degrees. Medical records only rarely give a duration for these baths, but they could last for up to twelve hours!

Although hydrotherapy was the general panacea, there were also other common practices. Leeches and bleeding aimed to relieve the body of excess blood. Leeches were applied to the thighs and the vulva. There were sometimes accidents. If leeches got into the vagina, douches with salt water were advised. Leeches were commonly used at the Salpêtrière throughout the nineteenth century. In 1870, Dr Chairon, chief of the medical staff at Le Vésinet asylum, recommended their use on the cervix to relieve the left ovary. But this was unusual.

At the Salpêtrière, doctors only bled patients on rare occasions. The records do not indicate which part of the body was bled, how much blood was taken or how often the treatment was carried out. It was probably prescribed when periods should have started, presumably on a monthly cycle. But this practice did decrease as time went on. It is not clear whether this was because alienists introduced a distinction between menstrual blood and blood from the rest of the body. Did the reproductive function of periods allow them to make a distinction once and for all between them and their male counterparts, haemorrhoids?

The result of these treatments determined the future of the patient in therapeutic terms. When periods started again, the alienists claimed victory. Since the cause had disappeared, it was only reasonable that madness would also decrease. If this did not happen, some doctors had very strange explanations, particularly if patients were paupers. These allegedly cured women were accused of malingering. The hospice aspect of asylums apparently explained why they wanted to stay there. In reality this highlights the problems faced by doctors when the facts contradicted their theories. Often they attributed the failure to be cured to the fact that patients had come on to their wards too late in the development of the illness. Their madness had become chronic and no longer needed to be explained in terms of periods. It was now autonomous. The result of treatment – that is the return of the menstrual cycle – was already an admirable achievement, but concomitant causes were now confusing the picture and hindering recovery.

The determination of the special doctors to defend their theories against all odds had serious consequences. The appearance and disappearance of periods were key factors in the development of any mental illness and the sure barometer of whether or not the patient could be cured. If periods returned, but no mental improvement took place, it was seen to mean that the patient was incurable. According to Brière de Boismont, the patient was definitely incurable if the return of periods was accompanied by renewed appetite and weight gain. The immediate consequence of the diagnosis would involve transfer to provincial asylums. Here treatment was no longer given.

The struggle against anorexia

'The refusal to eat' is how anorexia was described at the time. It was very common in women patients and exposed them to an ingenious variety of therapies. Their aim was as much to treat the symptoms and avoid the danger of malnutrition as to put an end to abnormal, undisciplined and anti-social behaviour. A very unequal struggle between doctor and patient ensued. The doctor's first task was to make patient open her mouth. This could be done with a flat steel spatula. The jaws were separated, then this was slipped under the molars. A small steel lever could then be placed vertically between the molars. When the spatula was removed, a stronger and larger wooden lever was introduced and pushed on to the tongue. The food, usually soup, was then poured in. When it was not possible for patients to take food normally, doctors used feeding tubes through the throat. The shape and the material from which they were made was the subject of various experiments which were often dangerous. Leuret devised a permanent feeding tube made of superimposed layers of sheep-gut. His trials in 1847 were not as successful as he had hoped. Alienists were concerned about the risk of accidents, and preferred to use Baillarger's oesophagal tube, furnished with a double chuck and a closing valve. Mealtimes for anorexics saw the use of a whole range of devices: the bottle gag, the silver mouth, the feeding bottle, the stomach key, the 'wooden duck', the bridle, the stomach pump and the spatula . . . a daily dose of horror.

REPRESSING SEXUALITY

The treatment of madwomen meant, of course, repressing their sexuality, forbidding its expression in any exaggerated forms and, specifically, denying the patients any sexual satisfaction. Once again, hysterical women, nymphomaniacs and erotomaniacs were not distinguished from masturbators. This confusion was current in all asylums. Despite the progress made in medical classification, medicine saw all these as sexual deviations and as pathological phenomena. The aim of doctors was to reduce all deviant sexual behaviour to a predisposing physical factor. If women could be shown to be physically mad, their free will vanished. Baillarger reported the case of Miss C, a twenty-four-year-old erotomaniac, who spent her days lying on her back with her legs apart so that her thighs would not come together and give her sensations which made her feel guilty. She was constantly struggling against the blood which she felt boiling in her belly. She felt that her cervix was about to collapse. The patient had to be vigilant:

> I have had . . . very strong sensations which spread everywhere, and which made me feel unbelievably calm and peaceful. To fight them I worked continuously, often from five in the morning until nightfall. I was entirely absorbed in what I was doing. I did not allow myself the little extra sleep I needed during the middle of the day because, as soon as I wanted to sleep, the sensations became so strong that I felt guilty about putting myself in a position where they might arise.[16]

Miss C's guilt gave hope for a cure, in Baillarger's view. If the opposite were true, and physical illness were added to mental illness, there would be only minimal chance of a cure. Doctors ranged in their accounts from scientific, clinical tableaux to discriminatory descriptions where pity and disgust turned their patients into 'poor creatures, unfortunate women, monsters'.

Obviously, onanism, that dreadful practice, was violently condemned. Its frequency in women was attributed to a perverted upbringing. Governesses were accused of resorting to these practices to calm down crying children. Girls' boarding schools were seen as breeding grounds for this evil. Traditional tales about the physical consequences of masturbation were long-lived. While Tissot's work on onanism continued to be read, the *Annales médico-psychologiques* spread its ideas.

In this journal, we can read about women 'victims' of masturbation who can be recognized by the bluish tinge about their eyelids, their digestive and circulatory problems, their lassitude and their thinness. The same picture was painted by Trélat, that of 'a woman at the age of thirty-six who looked as though she were fifty. She was prematurely bald, and one could only feel repelled and ashamed when one saw her wide-open, expressionless eyes, her empty head and heart and the lines of debauchery on her forehead.'[17] But these were only the first symptoms. They were followed by nervous afflictions, epilepsy and, in the worst cases, mental illness. This was usually in the form of lypemania. The patient's basic emotional constitution was also affected; it was replaced by 'monstrous perversions'.[18] Pursuing this monstrous practice when one was actually mad made the illness worse, caused spinal problems and could lead to complete paralysis. In the case of men it reduced chances of a cure, but 'for women, it was an insurmountable obstacle to renewed health.'[19] Masturbation needed to be treated in proportion to its gravity. Shock therapy was called for. Apart from the ubiquitous hydrotherapy, physically coercive methods gave alienists complete power over women's bodies. Straitjackets, bonds and handcuffs deprived the inmates of any freedom of movement. The apparatus used against these dire practices could reach heights of sophistication, pieces of cork tied to the inside thigh in order to prevent any exciting stimulation; special underwear was designed for each sex, closing at the back with a complex system of straps, laces and buckles.

If this anti-masturbatory equipment failed, the only way to silence sexuality was to kill it. The *Annales* quoted the report of Dr Legros to the Medical Society of the Temple in 1847 on two cases of clitoral amputation as a 'cure' for masturbation. Dr Legros decided to call this infamous practice 'clitorism'. The two operations were successfully conducted by Dr Robert. The first was carried out on a young woman; the result was very positive because the patient was cured of this vicious practice and able to get married. Encouraged by this success, Dr Robert repeated the operation ten years later on another young woman. He made it less painful this time by using ether.

Outdated definitions of hysteria also persisted. The identification of hysteria with nymphomania with erotomania makes it possible to measure the resistance of the alienists to new ideas. It seems that the walls of the asylums were too thick to let through new scientific and philosophical discoveries, even though hysteria was a fashionable subject. Books, theses and debates multiplied as people sought to define the illness. Research focused on two areas. First, the localization of the seat of hysteria, and then an investigation of why it only affected women. Gradually, the Hippocratic theory was abandoned and other organs in the genital sphere were made responsible. This widening of diagnosis emphasized the relationship between hysteria and gender, but reduced women's guilt. Thus, and in spite of basic differences, Dr Landouzy, the defender of this new approach, anticipated the work of Briquet.

Briquet's treatise swept away all the stereotypes. This marked the end of the theory of hysteria as a peculiarly female complaint and the end of the theory of sexual continence as the breeding ground of hysteria. It also marked the demise of the school of thought which saw sexual excess as responsible. The image of woman as a devouring and insatiable sexual organ was gradually being destroyed. Nymphomania came to be separated from hysteria. The origin of hysteria therefore had to be found elsewhere and the alienists turned their attention to the brain. Its balance was thought to be disturbed by passions. Briquet's position was revolutionary in two ways. Not only did he revolutionize the study of hysteria by separating it from other areas of investigation, but he also attempted an overall redefinition of femininity. It was a commonplace of the early nineteenth century that hysterics were no different from other women – only more extreme. This argument from nature was entrenched into a providential teleology which shares its aims with those of bourgeois society: 'Women had to be very emotionally receptive to fulfil their great and noble mission. They had to be able to feel everything within themselves. Just as all that is evil has its roots in good, hysteria unfortunately has its origins in this emotional receptivity.'[20]

Women were no longer guilty of hysteria, but it was a sign of their inherent inferiority. The male medical profession burdened women with the supposed glory of motherhood. They codified the division of roles between the sexes which already existed in society, and made all women potential hysterics: 'Every woman has the ability to feel, and this is already halfway to hysteria.'[21]

This potential was frequently realized, since it was not easy for women to escape the onslaught of a variety of predisposing and determining causes – gender, age, heredity, physical constitution, moral disposition, climate, social position, locality where primary education took place, type of education, diet, passions, moral inclinations, profession, sexual continence, menstruation and morbid states. Women were hardly likely to get away from this battery of conditions. Briquet somehow managed to demonstrate that the illness could affect men as well as women, but a few pages on, that it was a 'woman's prerogative'.[22] Men could not really be described as hysterics. True, a man expresses his passions through violence if he is strong, and through 'concentrated anger or depression if he is weak'.[23] These men might become hypochondriac, epileptic or mad, but not hysterical – or at least if they did become hysterical it was because they had a feminine temperament and were affected in the way women normally were. Excessive emotion could stop a man from playing his real role – that of the gallant knight. Hysteric men are unnatural, therefore. Briquet's account ends with an apotheosis: 'An hysterical man stands for the reversal of the constituted laws of society.'[24] Despite this, uterine theories remained fashionable. Some fifteen years later, Charcot recalled Briquet's ideas.

This time lag is significant. The attachment to these *a priori* judgements was linked to the desire not to threaten existing fantasies. In 1866, Jules Falret located his 'reasoning madness' in the tradition of misogyny. For him, hysterics are neither ill nor suffering but merely playing a part and living a lie. Although they are not really ill, they were thought to be completely anti-social deviants, all the more dangerous for hiding behind the masks of piety and devotion. 'They pass as saints while at the same time giving themselves over to the most shameful actions. In their homes, in front of their husbands and children, they create the most violent scenes using coarse and obscene language and they lead a disorderly life.'[25]

These lascivious women had to be kept in check within the walls of the asylum. This is indeed just what happened. During the hysteria epidemic at Morzine from 1857 to 1872, the 'demonics' had to be beaten by the police after the village had been surrounded by the authorities.[26] In these cases hydrotherapy showed its true face. The immersion and cold showers came complete with sermons. The words which recurred in what the alienists said were 'shame, dishonour for your family, bad behaviour'. They sounded more like priests than doctors.

To control fits a very limited range of drugs was used as well as water. Briquet prescribed chloroform; a wad of linen soaked in chloroform was placed under the nose of the hysterics. After vain attempts to push it away, the patients calmed down. Their muscles relaxed, they fell asleep and their convulsions stopped. But chloroform was only effective for fits of medium severity, and its usefulness was all the more limited since chloroform was dangerous. Doctor Lubin recommended injections of chloroform into the uterus through a tube. In 1860, he used eau-de-vie instead. Other drugs used in the treatment of hysteria included valerium, belladonna and ether. These were little used since many asylums had poor stocks of such drugs. When it was opened, the pharmacy at Sainte-Anne contained opium, potassium bromide and tincture of digitalis with opium. Drugs were used indiscriminately for agitation, insomnia, uterine infections and puerperal fevers. The stocks were always low. Alienists did not really mind, however, since they did not believe in drugs. Each had his own pet recipe. Baillarger and Legrand du Saulle believed in a milk-based diet for the treatment of hysteria-related mania. At Rodez, Doctor Combes made up a potion based on red wine, ground cassia amara in sugar, water clover, 80 per cent proof alcohol and gentian root.

When all else failed, solitary confinement was available to calm down these patients whose gender had made them mad. Was it to calm them down, or to get them out of the way? The latter was certainly the case with the lesbians, who terrified the doctors. They were quite unable to understand female sexuality and the nature of relationships between women. Pinel himself, the great liberator of the insane, thought that after all methods of repression had failed the only solution was 'to confine these victims of debauchery in remote cells, and leave them to wallow in the filth which their depraved imaginations dreamt up, without infecting others.'[27]

What conclusions can be drawn from this gallery of horrors to which madwomen were subjected in a very real sense? These treatments are an integral part of the asylum's war on deviants. To this extent they are not particularly misogynist. A cursory glance at the medical records relating to men shows that similar practices were carried out for male sexual deviants. But, and there is a but, there was less tolerance towards women. They were, then, more easily subject to the extremist rule of law found within the asylum.

It was impossible for the madwomen, already weakened by

their illness, to understand the 'coherence' of alienist thinking and to trust the doctor who ordered these treatments. Doctors and inmates did not understand each other's language. How could their worlds meet?

6

CONTACTS

The brutality of the madwoman's first contact with the asylum was followed by a whole series of confrontations. The primary evidence affords us only the odd glimpse of the reactions to daily life inside the institutions. Resistance to internment took four different forms. First, there was clearly expressed opposition which came in the form of a letter complaining about the committal; next came rebellion against the authorities; then escapes and attempted escapes; finally, general misbehaviour which expressed their feelings but affected the inmates themselves – for example, anorexia, mutism and attempted suicide.

There are only a few surviving examples of the first type of opposition in the archives. This is probably because of censorship by the medical staff. It was generally the male patients who protested in this way. However, we do have the case of a request to the Minister of the Interior from Descat-Bertin, a widow committed to Charenton, dated 6 August 1846. This patient sought to show that her long captivity, which had been the result of a slanderous letter, was unjustified. She very respectfully begged the Minister to answer her directly. She had been committed thirty-two years previously and had spent the time in a cell in a straitjacket. This is why she had not requested the Minister's help any earlier.

On the whole, women were more often silent than men. They seem to have accepted more readily the sentence passed by the authorities. They were also more often illiterate, another obstacle to an appeal by letter. This female passivity explains the rarity of violent attacks on asylum staff and the small number of attempted escapes. Sucessful escapes were even more rare. Celestine was officially committed to the Salpêtrière on the 3 March 1841. She made many attempts to escape, and succeeded after 137 days in the hospital. There were statistically more attempts at escape from

Bicêtre, and they were more successful, probably because of the physical strength of the male inmates. In 1839, ten inmates managed to escape from this hospital. Nationally, the number of escapes in any one year would be around one hundred, but we cannot tell how many of these were women. In times of political disturbance the disorganization on the wards showed itself in an increase in the number of escapes: 205 in 1871, for example.

It is not possible to ascertain whether or not suicide was part of mental illness, or a way of escaping confinement. Or, indeed, how these two factors interacted. Yet the small numbers of female suicides which we have already noted outside the asylums may be seen as an expression of the fact that women were basically resigned to their fate. From 1854 to 1860, forty-five female inmates killed themselves in French asylums, as opposed to seventy-one men. Most women gave in to medical power – but what did this power entail?

The decline of absolute medical power

Asylums were the places where special doctors could exert their authority on mental illness. To be fully effective, this power, in itself a therapeutic tool, had to be absolute and indivisible. Anything which diminished it would confuse the lunatics. Patients anticipated, hoped for or feared the arrival of Doctor. The asylum timetable was based on work, but for the patients the day was structured around the time when the alienist arrived. 'The Doctor's on his way, he is about to make his rounds.' This is how they expressed both their anticipation of the doctor's visits, and their disappointment at their brevity. He was a 'shooting star' who had to see everything, hear everything and organize everything but lacked the time necessary to do it. Esquirol wanted the doctor to live with the patients, and Ferrus had to admit that, mathematically, it would take several years of study for the doctor to get to know his patients well.

In 1872, after many improvements, there was only one doctor for 327 patients at the Salpêtrière. This was an insurmountable obstacle to any real contact between doctor and patient. Doctors, far from making contact easier, kept their distance from the inmates. Medical visits were not opportunities for meeting the patients; their purpose was the imposition of respect and order. The military element was stronger than the medical. Madwomen had to stand in silence in a row in the dining hall, or next to their beds. They had to get up as the doctor walked in and bare their heads. The alienist then reviewed his troops. He listened to reports on each patient from the general supervisor, which had been obtained from the supervisor of each section, which had in turn been obtained from the nurse-warders. The doctor based his prescription on these reports. He gave advice, prescribed drugs, gave encouragements, promised rewards, threatened and punished. Sometimes these punishments took place on the spot – sometimes showers, and sometimes just dousings with cold water. In general, except in the hydrotherapy rooms, the alienist was invisible, present everywhere as a threat but physically absent from daily life. This was the only direct encounter between doctor and patient.

The medical world responded to the challenge of madness, but did not accept that this meant contact with the insane. The relationship between the knowledge and the power of the medical elite and the degrading reality of mental illness had to be protective and mediating. Real and immediate physical power was in the hands of the staff at the bottom of the hierarchy who actually lived with the patients. They carried out the basic policing functions of the asylum. The total number of staff was small. At Fains there were eleven sisters in 1842: three sisters with six lay nurses looked after the ninety-one women inmates, with eight servants to do the basic work and act as wardens. As it was a mixed asylum, there was also a male gardener, a commissionaire, a mason and a carpenter; these backed up the sisters but were never supposed to come into contact with the mentally ill. At the Salpêtrière a great effort was made to increase the numbers of auxiliaries. This number went from 134 in 1834 to 140 in 1849 and 151 in 1852, or one member of staff per 9.27 patients, as opposed to one member for 6.66 at Bicêtre.

This limited staff was very hierarchical. Status was related to job. Those who actually looked after patients were at the top of the scale. These 'medical' staff despised the other workers, the laundresses, nursing auxiliaries and cooks who effectively ran the asylum. The so-called medical staff drew their status from their alleged knowledge, although in reality they frequently had no training whatsoever. This did not stop them from prescribing treatments. Sheltering behind a lie, they repressed and silenced their patients. The asylum offered staff the easy opportunity of satisfying their lust for power. In doing this, a climate of jealousy, envy and suspicion was created among the medical staff themselves. Various reports attacked the role of the auxiliaries who acted as a barrier between doctors and patients. What shocked the inspectors was not so much the impossibility of dialogue between the two worlds – this was a part of the structure of the asylum – but the fact that it meant robbing the doctors of some of their absolute power. This concern led to mutual suspicion. First of all, asylums began to lock up staff and patients together. A letter of 20 March 1857 commanded that employees living in the hospital should only enter and leave at times fixed by the director. The director himself had to live within the hospital and was not allowed to be absent for more than two days without the authorization of the Minister of the Interior.

The asylum village was born. A village implies clans, alliances, gossips, intrigues and plots. The doctors agreed on this: managing the warders was far more difficult than managing the patients!

Recruitment policy was often to blame. Many of the staff consisted of old inmates and there was always the risk of a relapse. They were torn between loving and hating the asylum which had become their home. The rigid structure governing the nurses and the nursed sustained this ambiguity. Girard de Cailleux was called the Chief Lunatic.

Although it was possible to dismiss lay staff, the presence of nuns made matters much more complicated. There were many clashes between secular and ecclesiastical staff. Nuns argued that they had been there before the doctors, and refused to obey them. They had been used to running these institutions, often before they had become special hospitals, and felt excluded from the new organization. These conflicts tended to simmer on and hindered the proper administration of medical treatment. Sometimes the situation would explode. At Fains, the sisters of Saint-Charles flatly refused to apply the law of 1838. On the advice of the chaplain, they refused to recognize the director's authority, which they held to be 'tyrannical and abusive'. They only obeyed the Mother Superior. Renaudin had to lance this boil. In 1845 the chaplain was recalled because of his subversive behaviour. The sisters abandoned the hospital, which was then taken over by the sisters of Saint-Vincent-de-Paul.

Nuns remained a problem. Some inspectors praised their patience, hard work and charity, but ended by reminding them that they were only nurses. They would not accept that the alienist was a special doctor. Some reports refer to the fear of the madwomen felt by religious staff and this is used to explain their lack of control over the patients. Sometimes the medical directors praise themselves for not being subject to such prejudices. Thus the power structures within asylums were manipulated by people with little or no knowledge, and asylums were essentially populated only by women.

A world of women, run by men

The asylum claimed to be totally genderless. Staff were expected to forget about gender differences. Nuns' habits underlined this asexuality. The fact that men were not allowed to work on the women's wards created an artificial female world. Women plotted and intrigued together, as in prisons, but patients might also forge alliances with each other and showed the kind of solidarity one sees among the oppressed in the face of their oppressors. In her memoirs, Hersilie puts herself forward as the representative of her companions. The inmates seemed concerned about the fate of the woman they called 'Punchinella'. In return, Hersilie used her influence with paying patients to protect her friends from punishment: 'The ladies refused to go to Vespers, and preferred to stay with me. I could see that this angered Sister Emilienne, the chief supervisor of the hospital. I put on my garden hat, saying that I would also go to Vespers, and everybody followed me.'[1]

Once again, the sources are incomplete. We cannot measure the extent of this kind of solidarity network in opposing the medical staff, or, indeed, in the face of the inevitable competition for the favours of the medical staff. It was easy for doctors to criticize but they were not the ones constantly facing explosive violence. Any pretext could unleash a violent incident which might precipitate rebellion. The removal of a pail of water placed there for the convenience of patients provoked an insurrection against Julie, a frightening and authoritarian nun. Hersilie tells the story:

> During break, we asked for water and I was given the task of going to get it. The servants locked in the kitchen were eating and I waited in the pantry. Julie came out.
> 'I'm thirsty,' I told her very brusquely. 'I'm thirsty, we are all thirsty, and there's not a drop of water to drink.'
> 'Just a moment', she said.
> 'We are thirsty, and we want some water, not in your own good time, but straight away. You can't deny lunatics their water!'
> Julie got frightened. She rushed to turn on the tap and fill a bucket, but the women rushed forward with such rage that the bucket was knocked over while another was being filled. The nearest and most thirsty woman put her whole head into the bucket to

drink. Her neighbours pulled at her dress so that they could drink too. The second bucket was overturned. It was an extraordinary scene – an unimaginable disruption . . . Julie was petrified, and took it on herself to fill the two buckets as usual, to avoid any more riots of this kind. She explained to the sister what had happened, and described the *demand* I had made on behalf of my companions. The next morning, the sister got the doctor to agree to transfer me, because they couldn't *throw me out*.[2]

Violence bred violence, sparking off the next round of repressive measures. It went beyond any therapeutic pretexts. Inspectors attacked the coercion and confinement administered by staff acting on their own initiative. Unjustified restraint was always blamed on the nurses, according to our sources. For example, in the case of the hospital of Saint-Lazare in Marseilles, Aubanel had to demand that the nuns should release patients as the inspector had requested. In fact doctors understood these tensions and often excused the excesses. Bertier recognized that 'our sisters are not angels, our supervisors are not saints.' He was convinced that 'many poor people could be treated much worse even in their families by clumsy or inexperienced people.'[3] The danger increased the lower down one went in the staff hierarchy. Divide and rule was the motto of the nurse-warders who incited dissension among the lunatics while retaining control over them. At Orléans, Hersilie was wounded by 'the stones thrown by these poor women who were completely mad and did not know what they were doing. They hit with their clogs, scratched me and spat in my face.'[4]

The margin for manoeuvre among the servants increased as medical power diminished. It was only balanced by the presence of the nuns. In the 1850s the alienists chose to replace lay people with religious staff. They agreed with Renaudin, who held that 'the institutions are good or bad depending on whether they are well or badly administered, and especially on the amount of intrigue allowed to develop.' The most important quality and fault of the nuns was their womanhood. In 1863 the directors of Fains made the following recommendations: 'we must use their excellent qualities, and guard against the faults inherent in their sex. Our patients love and respect the sisters, and the families trust their sensitive nursing.' Renaudin did recognize that there were abuses, as a result of the weakness of the leadership or of 'the flatteries which so many people lavished on the staff'.[5] This was dangerous, because there was frequently no leadership at all. At Orléans, there were no housemen. The morning visits were carried out by the chief doctor. The sisters moved from one job to another and it was the servants who trained them. These servants, according to Hersilie, formed a coherent group who neglected the care of patients while they sat and gossiped.

At Aix-en-Provence, the institution was run in 1843 by a Mother Superior. There were no medical staff and the non-resident doctor very rarely went to the asylum. The power lay in the hands of the seven members of staff. This was an unusual situation. It was more common for the lord of the manor to rule over his serfs. This was the second feature of women's asylums. They did not merely consist of women, but were governed by *one* man. Or sometimes two, if the doctor was not also the director. This was a unique situation. The power of the alienist was multiplied in cases like this and therefore a sexual dimension was introduced into asylum life. Because of his sex and the power that he held, the doctor was the target for what we would call today 'transference' and projected fantasies. The hospital records have little to say about this but it is clear that the inmates understood the political structure of asylums. The special doctor was explicitly called Lord and Master by some inmates. Patients knelt before him, or wanted to kiss their Lord's hand. This stimulated romantic fantasies. The alienist was the husband figure, but rarely a father; in those cases, he would become a fantasy figure – the King, the Husband and Master.

When the inmates were still lucid, they would understand their own position of inferiority in relation to the doctors. They would address the alienist with deference and submission and beg for his mercy as if he were a judge:

> Doctor, Sir, I beg you, do not be angry with me. Please talk to me. I am a poor creature who needs indulgence and pity, not severity. I have been parted from the mother I love. Haven't I been punished enough for my misdemeanours in my family? Soon, Sir, if you would be so kind as to give me this great honour, I will ask to speak to you for a few moments, alone, because I have very important things to discuss with you.[6]

The image of the doctor also encouraged religious monomanic fantasies. The alienist was seen as God, sometimes the Sun. In spite of anything he might do, he was never seen as the devil, although he was sometimes responsible for the sufferings of the patient. In those cases he was an avenging God. Patients tended, then, to use doctors as a way of reinforcing their own neuroses. Gossip had it that women were sexually aggressive towards their doctors. It is very difficult to separate truth from fiction here.

None of our witnesses is credible enough to confirm or deny the descriptions of inmates' alleged erotic behaviour. A few stray pieces of information give us some idea of the nature of the possible relationships between female patients and 'the man in their lives'. Occasionally inmates accused doctors of abusing them. The records treat such reports as a part of the erotic delirium which had led to the confinement in the first place.

There is also the case of a conflict between Hersilie and Dr Auzouy. After a night in which she sweated profusely (because, she claimed, of the menopause), Hersilie gave her underwear to a nurse. While she waited for her new clothes, she covered herself with two petticoats, a woollen scarf and a shawl. When the Mother Superior told the doctor that the patient was not wearing any underwear, the doctor burst into her room. A sister and two nurses stripped Hersilie and tied her up in a straitjacket. The medical 'commando' then apparently tore up all Hersilie's clothes. When things had returned to normal, the patient asked for paper to write to the minister. Auzouy then ran to the director, M. Barroux, claiming that Hersilie wanted to prosecute him for 'indecent assault'.

Accusations of indecent assault, of sexual provocation or even of rape were an integral part of life in the asylum and affected all relationships. Auzouy apparently told Hersilie when she arrived that she would not be able to seduce him. We have already seen the severe repression with which alienists treated nymphomaniacs and erotomanics because they were frightened and disgusted by these women. The aura of the bewitching temptress pervaded the asylum. Doctors withdrew from these disturbed and disturbing seductresses by keeping their distance. Jeanne was committed to Trélat's ward. She complained about her committal to her father in harmless letters, accusing him of preferring visits to the countryside to coming to see her in the asylum. Trélat believed that Jeanne had no moral sense, and put on a single level her incestuous desires, her alleged lasciviousness (she had had sexual relationships with several men) and her greed. He disregarded the fact that she desperately needed to be loved and saw her frantic quest for love as a pathological symptom. The lack of affection she felt led her from one perversion to the next. According to Trélat, she wrote to a woman assistant in a previous ward to declare her love.[7]

The alienist was frightened by this type of patient and made quite sure that he was not left alone with them, particularly after Jeanne had chosen the doctor as the confidante she needed to

express the sufferings of her heart. An integral part of the
alienist's role was to keep his distance from his patients. This was
necessary because of his status and because of the degeneration
caused by madness. They refused the marks of affection which
patients wanted to bestow. When a patient leaving the Salpêtrière
was leaving the hospital, she asked Trélat to kiss her forehead to
say goodbye. He agreed to do this through a nun. This example
also shows how patients liked and trusted their doctors. According
to the alienists it took a long time to earn this trust; even if it
existed, it was very rarely expressed. Indifference was the
dominant feeling in asylum life. A strong impetus was needed
before patients could break through the emotional restraints.
Transfers could act as detonators. Some inmates wept at losing
their doctors. Others refused to speak to them and told the nuns
to convey 'their best wishes' to the psychiatrist. These examples
set matters straight. Imprisonment, torture and solitary confinement were not the general rule, however common they may have
been.

In 1844, at the Avignon hospital run by the sisters of Saint-
Joseph, a nun, Clémence Olivier, was found chained up in a
narrow dungeon with a chain fixed about ninety centimetres up
on the wall.[8] She was wearing a straitjacket and lying face down
on straw fouled with excrement. Because of her mental state she
was transferred to the Royal Infirmary. Anonymous lines in the
Indicateur d'Avignon accused the administrators of sequestration.
The prefect of Vaucluse asked for a report about her case. The
article in the *Indicateur* claimed that, contrary to what the director
had said, the patient was not allowed any visits. Although visits
were not allowed, the anonymous writer managed to see her and
observed that there was no improvement in her condition. She
continued to think that her name was 'potato', 'bean' or 'Belise',
she chewed dry leaves gathered in the courtyard and was incontinent. The writer sought to gratify his readers hungry for
sensation by claiming that the woman was homicidal and had
tried to strangle two nuns. The alienist's report stated that she had
not been sequestered, and that she had been receiving visitors in
accordance with the law of 22 October 1842. He stressed the
progress she had made. Her physical condition had improved,
the oedema on her lower limbs had vanished and she could now
move freely. Her mental state had improved slightly. Clémence
now showed some modesty. Her gestures were less lewd and she
answered questions a little more precisely. As for the homicidal
tendencies which had been reported, they were the distortion of

an insignificant incident in which she had tried to save herself from falling by holding on to the neck of a nurse. This had been exaggerated by a malicious individual.

The minor incidents of everyday life could clearly be wildly exaggerated – and the press loved to do this. Yet the medical and philanthropic press both justly praised alienists. The staff, they would say, were devoted and patient in their care for the inmates, who were, it should be remembered, totally rejected by the rest of society.

And if an inmate thought she was being victimized, she had one final solution. She could call in the inspectors.

The last resort: the inspectors

If her letters of complaint remained unanswered, the inmate's only hope was to rely on the vigilance of the inspectors and other visitors. She had to be bold enough to speak out and explain her predicament. This final resort, which involved appealing to a man, required a good deal of courage. The inspector's role made him unapproachable, and the hospital staff stood between him and the inmates. It was the staff who organized meetings, or made sure that they did not happen. As for the inspectors, they were less worried about the patients than about the institutions. Inspections focused on whether the administrative aspects of the law of 1838 were being carried out; they only focused on the living conditions, and the possibility of inhuman treatment, in the last instance. Their main concern was to fight against the exploitation of the inmates as unpaid labour for non-therapeutic purposes or for any tasks which didn't contribute to making asylums self-sufficient. Directors were absolutely forbidden to abuse this potential workforce by ruthlessly using patients as their own domestic staff.

Inspections were rarely unexpected. The dice were loaded. When they were announced, there was turmoil, and this always bitterly amused Hersilie. When Parchappe arrived at Maréville, 'the entire asylum had been cleaned from top to bottom and everyone was in high spirits. The patients were dressed in their party clothes, there were flowers in the workrooms and an orchestra with a choir welcomed the Inspector.'[9]

When the inspectors arrived unannounced, the premises were rarely as welcoming as this. Maréville had this experience when Girard de Cailleux arrived: 'He came like a bomb, without warning, and the institution was unprepared. It was neither clean nor decorated. Maréville had been caught short. What a shambles! What a disgrace for the asylum!'[10]

It was always easy for the doctor showing the inspector around to direct his steps and to push aside any troublemakers. In any case, listening to the patients was hardly the most important aspect of the visit. The presence of a Stranger, Judge and Inquisitor, with the dreaded doctor present at his side, silenced many a patient.

They were afraid of possible repercussions. If the inmates did dare to speak, the inspector would weigh their words against those of the alienists. The women were bound to lose; the men were united. This was part of an alliance which implicitly linked doctors from different hospitals. It was seen as tactless, or at least unwise, to free a woman whom one of your colleagues had diagnosed as mad; it was better to wave a wand and claim that the committal had been justified, but that the patient was now suddenly cured. This professional solidarity led to unofficial links between wards in different asylums. Patients were transferred in order to resolve conflicts; others were kept where they were in order to 'save one's colleagues trouble'.[11] Dr Payen went as far as to pretend that he 'was devoted to helping his colleagues',[12] and more specifically, to helping Trélat.

This spirit of solidarity impeded the operation of the law of 1838. Hersilie, registered under the incorrect name of Chevalier, was one victim. Although this mistake was recognized, she remained alienated from her own property, and the sacred links between doctors were preserved. The doctors closed ranks over Hersilie's lawsuit. The *Annales medico-psychologiques* preferred to remain silent, but *La France médicale* counter-attacked. In its issue of 12 August 1871, Dr Laurens (a former chief asylum doctor) refused to believe that patients could be committed arbitrarily. Even more interesting, he denied the possibility that anyone other than a special doctor could assess the truth of what an ex-patient might say. Dr Laurens refused to acknowledge any weakness in the system; consequently he was the spokesman for a group which refused to concede any of its power whatsoever. As Laurens noted, 'after the Commune the prestige of the alienist doctor could not be stressed too highly.'[13] The doctor was there to protect society, which would be demoralized without his advice.

From hatred to indifference, love to trust – the whole range of human emotions was there in the asylum, though negative feelings predominated. Asylums were not places where one was cared for. Similarities with the prisons were obvious. Psychiatric inmates still retained some hope, and awaited their release, if not their cure. Inmates could not have ignored the fact, if they were at all lucid, that only about 15 per cent of them would ever leave. For the others, there was no end, except death.

The Endless Asylum or the End of the Asylum?

Incurable

This diagnosis was effectively a sentence. It was passed on one out of every two patients. This was decided either on arrival or within two years, when the doctors could see that the patient had not improved. Such a diagnosis could also be made when patients had, say, regained their appetite, or their periods had started again without any noticeable improvement in their condition. Immediately the asylum as a place for therapy would give way to the asylum as a place to live. The special hospitals looked after these women, trapped within their madness, and no longer treated them, beyond repressing any violent behaviour or preserving physical health. In Paris the verdict 'incurable' meant that patients would leave for provincial asylums. A stay of more than five years in a Parisian asylum was rare. These transfers would relieve pressure on the asylums but also symbolized defeat.

The first large-scale transfer took place at the Salpêtrière. Two hundred inmates were carted off from there to Saint-Venant in groups of twenty. It was a dangerous journey, made in a modified carriage. There was room for twelve passengers in all, including the frenetic and senile patients from the Baillarger wards. The calm and continent patients were on the bench at the back. Each seat had a hole and a pipe for disposal of bodily wastes. The back and underneath of the seats had iron rings on to which the strait-jackets and bonds were fixed. Iron bars had been fixed to the windows and the glass had been replaced by shutters. The mad-women were accompanied by an assistant warder and two staff. The convoy was officially under the authority of a deputy adminis-trator. The journey lasted thirty hours and was not too difficult. One patient who had eaten too much suffered from indigestion and the inmates on the bench complained of the cold. This peculiar convoy aroused the curiosity of the public, particularly when it stopped.

These inconveniences were dealt with the next time such a transfer took place. Eighteen patients from two wards left the Salpêtrière for Maréville some distance away. Five of them were in straitjackets. This journey was rather difficult, as Sister Sophie described in her report to Trélat:

> To begin with they were very agitated until one in the morning. Then several of them slept and all was calm until seven o'clock. From seven until nine there was chaos. Delettrez and Bertrand were trying to bite. I had to cover their heads for a few moments with my shawl and my apron. While I was helping an epileptic who was having a fit, Duval untied Pouget. I had great difficulty in tying her up again, because she resisted with all her strength. At the same time, we had to stop the carriage so I could put Lamirale into a straitjacket, because she was scratching and biting her companions.[1]

Trélat quite rightly worried about the problems caused by these transfers. Despite such incidents as these, he believed that the trip was beneficial (as were all breaks in the monotony of asylum life): the pleasure at departure, the affection shown by a patient towards a member of staff and the pre-emption of a crisis all proved that it was worthwhile. Yet this feeling sustained the illusion that going elsewhere meant escaping the wards inhabited by the incurables. Patients could put on new clothes and admire their new white calico petticoats, lifting up their new grey cloth dresses to look. It was an ephemeral pleasure. They were destined for another asylum – other faces, other buildings. When they arrived, they would cry and ask their new doctors if they could go back home. The Salpêtrière became a lost Eden. These requests were in vain. The transfer was not reversible. Patients were doomed to stay in their new asylum.

The directors of these asylums were the first to complain. In 1846 the director of the Blois asylum asked to be sent patients who could be treated. The director of the Maréville asylum reminded the authorities that these transfers were supposed to happen in exceptional circumstances only. They were also supposed to be temporary. In fact, from 1852 to 1858 the average length of committals was 3,301 days in provincial asylums as against 624 days at the Salpêtrière. This was because of the burden of incurable patients who were sometimes the only patients in the asylum – as at the asylum for the department of Orne in 1848. Occasionally patients would change asylums again either as a disciplinary measure or because the contract between the Parisian and the provincial asylum had not been renewed. The result was the same – patients would be totally forgotten. It was the fault of the Parisian authorities. Only patients who never had visitors were supposed to be transferred. In reality, many of those transferred were not alone in the world and would lose their last links with family and friends. Therefore, the level of release from the asylum by request from external sources was very low. Madwomen who might be incurable but were certainly not dangerous ended their days buried and forgotten in provincial asylums; from 1844 to 1858 only one in every 54.25 inmates was taken out of these asylums at their family's request while they were still ill. The level for the Salpêtrière was one in 11.16.

There was a worse side to this story. In provincial asylums, getting better did not necessarily mean release. The interests of the asylums were put before the patients, and although an incurable patient was a dead weight, she was also paid for by the department of the Seine at a higher rate than that for local patients within the department of the asylum. The fact that the Seine paid 1.25 francs per patient as opposed to the 60 centimes paid by the department of the Pas-de-Calais meant that Parisian patients were eagerly sought after. The authorities closed their eyes to this and often allowed patients who could have been cured to leave for the provinces. The level of bedridden patients (men and women) in Parisian hospitals was one in 4.5, as opposed to one in 12 in the provinces. The provincial hospitals wanted this labour force and Girard de Cailleux complained that with time Parisian asylums were becoming 'huge hospitals for the insane of the Seine'. As for those who were transferred, he gave them a motto taken from Dante: 'Abandon all hope, ye who enter here.'

Only a very few managed to cling on to the vain hope that they would one day leave the asylum.

Leaving

Leaving the asylum and being cured were not synonymous in the vocabulary of asylum life. Unfortunately the remaining records only rarely reflect this crucial distinction. The number of patients leaving asylums, usually at around the age of thirty-eight, decreased with time. Until 1844 they were about 16.7 per cent, then they fell to 13.9 per cent from 1846 to 1860. This was most probably because of the policy of transfers to provincial asylums. Being uprooted slowed down or stopped the process of remission and only about one in twenty of those forgotten patients in provincial asylums ever received any treatment. The poor quality of medical care and the general discouragement of doctors also kept the numbers of patients cured very low. Taking men and women together, one patient in 31.7 was cured and able to leave the provincial asylums from 1844 to 1858. In the same period of time, one in 3.34 people from the Seine were cured and released. This was lower than in the preceding period and can be explained by the lack of interest which alienists showed in patients who might at any moment be transferred.

It was also asylum policy to cut down on the release of patients. Given that official committals rose sharply and that from 1843 only paupers were treated for free, asylums filled up with people who were very severely ill and therefore more difficult to rehabilitate into society. Women were more affected than men. Out of 100 patients, 45 to 47 women would be released as opposed to 54 to 55 men. Madwomen were truly the victims of their emotional solitude, of their lack of training and therefore of money. Being able to work was one of the determining criteria for being allowed to leave the asylum. On humanitarian grounds, doctors preferred to keep patients in asylums rather than make them face insurmountable difficulties of rehabilitation. More than half of those kept in asylums were spinsters, and this number was sometimes higher in provincial asylums. Whatever their medical condition, the abandoned patients moved out to the provinces were very rarely released from hospital. The doctors were concerned that with nowhere to go the patients would become vagrants, particularly in the towns.

This was not surprising. When patients left the asylum they would find themselves alone, disorientated and without any money. They would have lost their accommodation and their furniture would probably have been sold. Their network of friends would have moved on. They would find themselves with nothing, needing to start again from scratch with the additional burden of their history of insanity uppermost in everyone's mind, although they were now cured. They had to find work, but: 'women with limited and thankless jobs, even if they are in the best of health, become victims of prejudice and unjust restrictions . . . Timid by nature and made even more timid because of their illness, they need to be encouraged.'[2] But asylums did not help those outside their gates. Doctors such as Dr Richard, the director of the Stephansfeld asylum, called on charity, the Church and even on science to 'give convalescents from mental illness the care and treatment which they had received in asylums.'[3] He called for help in re-establishing contact, dialogue and reconciliation between released patients and those around them.

The *Annales médico-psychologiques* praised any such actions: for example, the aid society of the lower Rhine region which, in 1843, was run by donations; the more ephemeral society of the asylum of Saint-Yon, and the aid society of Nancy founded by Morel to fight against degeneration. The *Annales* particularly praised those organizations which helped women, seen as being the most vulnerable. This preconception was contradicted by the statistics which show that only 48 per cent of women as opposed to 50 per cent of men had a relapse. At the Salpêtrière one in every ten women fell ill again. In theory at least, they were helped by two organizations set up in 1843, replacing the purely financial help, called the Montyon Fund, which was all that had existed up till that point. The Society for Care and Lodgings, which dealt with convalescents from the Salpêtrière, was founded by J-P Falret. At first it depended on the good will of the ladies who supported it. They were, on the whole, wives of doctors. On Wednesday mornings they awaited the release of impoverished patients and sought to resolve their immediate problems. They provided a hotel room for one night, or sent them to the Sisters of Charity at 35, Rue du Plumet. Here they could find temporary accommodation. These ladies also paid the fares of ex-patients who wanted to return home to the country. Finally, they tried to find jobs for their charges, mainly as domestic servants. Falret's system was gradually consolidated by the development of a network of influential supporters. Mgr Dupanloup, Parisian parish priests and the Sisters of Saint-Vincent-de-Paul supported the society, which eventually gained official recognition with the award of a grant. It finally received charitable status. From that point on, it was able to organize its own publicity to bring its work to public notice, and it could use some of its funds to set up lotteries for the benefit of former patients.

In 1847, it merged with the second organization that had come into existence, the Society for the Support of Madwomen from the Salpêtrière, also founded in 1843. This latter society sought to limit the risk of relapses into madness, as dangerous for society as they were for the women themselves because of the economic damage to society as it lost part of its workforce and gained a burden on its budget for aid. This society combined both humanitarian and economic motives, unlike the charitable emphasis of Falret's society, and as a result its assistance was mainly financial. Temporary allocations were drawn from the Montyon Fund after a decision taken by the General Council of Hospices on the 3 April 1844. Assistance was given to those who left the Baillarger wards. In one year the society helped 140 convalescents in this way. When the two societies merged, they were able to extend and reorientate 'care and housing for impoverished patients who left the public asylums of the department of the Seine as convalescents'. It sounds surprisingly modern – the emphasis was on help in the home, and crisis intervention aimed at avoiding committal. They paid regular visits to their clients, both male and female from this point onwards, and they were proud of the lives they had saved. Take Adelaïde for instance. She owed her landlord one year's rent, which she tried to pay with 'a promissory note signed by the imaginary demon who pursued her'. She was upset by his refusal to accept this and tried to throw herself out of a sixth floor window. The Mother Superior intervened, calmed her down and rescued her. Adelaïde thanked her profusely and blamed herself for forgetting that 'the asylum was her home'. She blessed the nun.[4]

These interventions were successful because it was possible to help convalescent women whose madness was lying dormant by putting them up 'in a house where they would be happier, with a garden where they could walk'.[5] In 1856 a workroom was set up by six nuns from the church of Notre-Dame de Gramat. It was so successful that it outgrew its premises and had to be restructured. On Sundays, the nuns would meet and advise the ladies who supported the cause, and guide them in the direction of those they were to help. Their philanthropic zeal diminished with time and the ladies became little more than fund-raisers. The real work was done by the congregation. Overwhelmed with work, they were not able to help all the released patients; in fact they could not help Hersilie. She ended up wandering the streets of Paris in a short-sleeved dressing gown embroidered with lace and pink ribbons, bare headed and in slippers.

In the provinces there were only localized attempts at providing this kind of assistance. The sole support offered on leaving the asylum was with obtaining passports, and financial help with travelling. In theory, this type of help did not need to be approved by the Minister of the Interior, and should have been automatic. In practice, this rarely happened. Despite all good intentions, private charities were not able to make up for the inadequacies of the public charities whose role they tried to take over. The reactions of those who did receive help towards their patrons is known only indirectly. The lurid stories which do emerge distort the real underlying picture of what might have been said.

But there was an even weightier silence – the silence of death.

Death

We have come full circle. There is no end to the asylum. Many patients died there and were buried there as if it were their home. Madwomen met again ultimately in death – they even joined members of the medical staff who had fallen honourably in the battle against madness. The morgue and the cemetery were slightly removed from the main part of the asylum and blended in with the landscape. Were patients frightened of this, or indifferent? We have no idea of what madwomen thought about death. Here even the doctors did not distort what they had to say – there is simply no evidence at all. Death silenced them. The alienists' works on the subject are rather impersonal. After reporting a death, they would set out the results of the autopsy. Doctors tended to search for possible organic causes for the madness. They state in almost all cases that such a cause is absent, except in congenital illnesses. The dryness of these reports is striking. The actual cause of death is never mentioned and we cannot tell if it was madness or a physical illness. In death, the lunatic immediately forfeited what small amount of humanity remained even in madness; they were swallowed up by statistics, became ciphers and impersonal numbers. We have no choice but to follow the path trodden by the special doctors in dealing with this subject.

The figures are impersonal but they do say something. The mortality rate in the asylum was six times higher than in the outside world. Between 1843 and 1853, one in 7.27 inmates died, as against one in 41 outside. We cannot quantify the number of cases where death was the result of madness, but it seems to have been a very small number. The main culprit was poor hygiene. This is why the mortality rate was higher in Parisian hospitals than in provincial asylums and private nursing homes. The alienists explained this in terms of olfactory theories. They blamed the mephitic vapours which patients breathed, rather than the general conditions in the special hospitals. These vapours were caused, they thought, by overcrowding in the asylum, and especially by the presence of senile and paralytic patients. Their breath, their sweat and their excrement were fetid; they seeped into the walls, contaminating the inhabitants. The lack of exercise and freedom were also cited as causes of death. From 1842 to 1860, there was little variation in the mortality rate. But epidemics also struck. In 1849, cholera killed 306 women at the Salpêtrière, one in four. Strangely enough, the paralytic patients were not affected. Among the staff, seventeen ward assistants and two doctors also perished. Other inmates who recovered from the cholera attack later died because of their lowered resistance to illness.

Charenton was not affected by cholera in 1849, but it was in 1854: eleven patients died in the first ten days. Years with a high death rate were followed by a fall, because the weakest patients had all died. Epidemics aside, chest infections were responsible for many of the deaths, and for the fact that they peaked in winter. According to Georget, consumption caused half the deaths in the Salpêtrière, and found easy targets in working-class women already ground down by lives of deprivation. Consumption was closely followed by pneumonia and scurvy. The improvement of living conditions and hygiene reduced the levels of scurvy and digestive diseases which had been particularly high in manic, monomanic and lypemanic patients. So-called incidental illnesses were more closely related to the behaviour of the patients. Manic patients suffered from inflammations of the vocal chords because of their singing and shouting. They were so restless that they often cut themselves – in fact these wounds ranged from simple bruises to deep gashes (caused by the metal bathtubs) or even more serious lesions. This also happened to monomanics; but they also suffered from fractures because they were not steady on their feet.

Staff supervision and restraint of patients helped to reduce fatal accidents. Men were more violent than women – thirty women died accidentally from 1854 to 1860, as against fifty-seven men. The women's deaths were mainly the result of asphyxiation when they choked on their food. Restraint could lead to ulcers, phlebitis and abcesses. Sores could become gangrenous, and this was one of the terrible risks associated with the uses of fetters and straitjackets. Obviously all these were not always fatal. Boils and carbuncles on the buttocks and breasts were even considered fortunate because they might alleviate madness. There were no illnesses specific to women, except amenorrhoea, which was, of course, not fatal. However, women were more resistant to asylums and their dangers than men. From 1842 to 1853, 45.82 per cent of deaths were in the women's wards, as opposed to 54.18 per cent among the men. Death claimed one out of every 6.44 women. This discrepancy between the sexes reflects the fact that women lived longer. In 1853 the average age of death was forty-eight years and one month; this was three years and eleven months later than the male average. Women were obviously better adapted to asylum life, although this is not a sufficient explanation for their relative longevity. Alienists believed this to be the result of their sedentary and monotonous lives. Solitary confinement, although praised, caused 19 per cent of the deaths in the Salpêtrière in 1853. Death usually struck during the first month of confinement. This figure is not easy to interpret because it includes patients committed when their madness was too far advanced for any cure to be possible.

Once patients had survived the first month, the death rate stabilized. It rose again after a year in hospital, and again, strongly, after two years, when illnesses became chronic and incurable. Forms of therapy and the structure of the asylums were less important than the nature of the asylum population. If most patients were old, as was often the case in provincial asylums, their resistance to epidemics was low. Elderly patients would also die of old age rather than the effects of madness. However, madness was an aggravating factor. There was also a relationship between the death rate, age and marital status: 14.9 per cent of deaths were of widows and widowers, as opposed to 7.01 per cent of single people, and 8.73 per cent of married people. There was no protection against death. Poverty weakened the patients and robbed them of their desire to fight. All madwomen ended their lives in poverty, and met a common fate beneath the earth of the asylum.

Conclusion

All the modern historian hears are these sighs, pleas and whispers from the past . . . cries and screams, too, which express the pain of madness and of incarceration. Yet the oppression of the asylum muffles the voices and sufferings of the women behind the distorting masks of madness. What they had to say was interpreted simply as transparently symptomatic of their illness, and a reaction to the miserable and confined world imposed on them.

The authoritative structure of the asylum system served only to reinforce women's madness. Pathologically, madness took the following main forms: mutism, anorexia and depression. Fits were sporadic and they tended to be violently self-destructive in response to feelings of guilt which the moralizing discourse of the special doctors constantly nurtured.

The special hospital was the only answer to many different forms of mental illness. Patients who today would receive various types of psychotherapeutic treatments were mixed together with deeply disturbed patients who needed psychiatric assistance. The inmates lost their identity and doctors did not respond to the specific nature of their illness. In practice, congenital, pathological mental illness has little in common with occasional emotional disturbances.

'Accidental' madness is a 'metalanguage' which can be read in the light of the life history of the inmates before committal. To understand it, we have had to tell the story of their lives and travel with them on the road from normality to madness. Their journey was fraught with obstacles placed there by a society which defined what was permissible in terms of male bourgeois culture. These rigid boundaries were fixed by a society which chose to ignore the fact that it was thereby forcing these women into madness. For the more sensitive or less pliant women, madness was the only escape from a world of pent-up frustrations and unrealizable longings. The 'acceptable' ways of life denied women the right to fulfilment, whether emotional, physical or intellectual, and allowed them no possible compensations for enduring the rigours of daily life. Many women's mental health gave way under the weight of domestic, emotional and socio-economic problems.

The common link between the mental illnesses we have described here inheres in the condition of women at the time. The illnesses were cultural rather than natural. This informs the face they presented both inside and outside the asylum.

As onlookers, we can observe the power relations between the inmates and the medical profession. Women projected on to the doctors their relationship to men and male power, distorted and deformed by illness. This projection was emphasized by the lordly behaviour of the doctors, but the real relationship was made more distant by the number of intermediaries between doctor and patients. In this way the alienists protected themselves against contagion and against their fear of the untameable female character. They held this responsible for madness in women, which they always managed to relate to a biological cause, often using fairly questionable pseudo-scientific arguments. Their basic implication was that all women were potentially mad. When we compare their analyses of clinical cases with the information given us by the records, we can see just how their prejudice distorted their medical judgement. The nascent science of psychiatry was still a prisoner of the tradition of the mad sex. Hysteria, nymphomania, and erotomania were disproportionately privileged. The current theories of causation sustained the most outmoded clichés, without at all upsetting the logical coherence of the alienists' theories.

Under these conditions, no dialogue between special doctors and madwomen was possible. Moral treatment was undermined. It no longer involved an attempt to understand madness, but became an attempt to constrain it in a world of poverty and material deprivation.

The asylum sought to force women back into the mould from which they had just tried to escape. Sick from lack of attention and understanding, women were supposed to be 'cured' without being either heard or understood. Behind the paternalistic philanthropy of the asylum there lurked violent forms of therapy whose aim was to silence women. Given therapeutic status, work and repression were the main agents of this form of control. To be cured meant to be passive and submissive. The image of healthy womanhood put forward by the special doctors, those products and exponents of bourgeois ideology, was of silent women who showed moderation in everything, and who sublimated all their own desires in their role as mothers.

Alienist science as applied to women was at its birth a socially coercive form of medicine. There can be little doubt that these beginnings had a major effect on the subsequent development of psychiatry and of psychoanalysis.

NOTES

For reasons of space, only pathological cases, and the quotations taken from medical records are included here. To guarantee the anonymity of the descendants of patients, first names and the names of patients have been changed. Their case histories came from hospital records; they are documented according to their date and the manner of admission. Series 'Q' in the records deals with admissions, series 'R' deals with the records of medical observations at the Salpêtrière. These documents may be consulted at the archives of the Assistance Publique. Series 'F' of the national archives, 'Hospices et secours', contains relevant papers deposited by the Ministry of the Interior. Technical words or words used in a specialized sense are explained in the glossary which follows.

Introduction

1 E. and J. Goncourt, cited by M. Juin in the preface to *Germinie Lacerteux*, 2nd edn, Paris 1979, p. 18.
2 Dr C. Lasègue, 'Notice nécrologique sur J.-P.Falret', in *Archives générales de médecine*, I, Paris 1871, p. 488.

Chapter 1   Outcasts from Society

1 Hersilie Rouy, *Mémoires d'une aliénée*, Paris 1883, pp. 88–9.
2 Ibid., p. 90.
3 F15 3903.
4 Dechambre, *Dictionnaire encyclopédique des sciences médicales*, I, under 'Assistance', Paris 1864–89, p. 622.
5 F15 3900.
6 Drs Constans, Lunier, Dumesnil, *Rapport général sur le service des aliénés en 1874 adressé à M. le Ministre de l'Interieur*, Paris 1878, p. 475.
7 Letter from the Chief of Police in Paris to the members of the Council

of Hospices,quoted in *Statistiques des établissements d'aliénés de 1842 à 1853 inclusivement*, Paris 1854, p. 6.

8 See the discussion of A. Corbin in *Les filles de noces, Misère sexuelle et prostitution au XIXième siècle*, Paris 1978, p. 443.

9 Salpêtrière, 6R3.

10 6Q2 4

11 6Q2 3.

12 6Q2 5.

13 *Annales médico-psychologiques*, XI, Paris 1848, pp. 346–58.

14 Rouy, *Mémoires*, pp. 201–2, original emphasis.

15 6R3.

16 Ulysse Trélat, *La folie lucide etudiée au point de vue de la famille et de la société*, Paris 1861, p. 187.

17 6R24.

18 Jules Vallès, *Tableaux de Paris*, Delphes, 1964 edn, pp. 61–2.

19 Etienne Esquirol, *De la lypémanie ou mélancolie*, Toulouse, 1977 edn, p. 129.

20 A. Brière de Boismont, 'De l'emploi des moyens coercitifs', discussion from the *American Journal of Insanity* in the *Annales médico-psychologiques*, VI, Paris 1871, pp. 125–6.

21 C. Stak, 'La dégenérescence du peuple français, son caractère pathologique, ses symptomes et ses causes. Contribution de médecine mentale à l'histoire médicale des peuples', with a bibliographical note by Morel, *Annales médico-psychologiques*, VI, Paris 1871, pp. 290–9.

22 Brière de Boismont, 'De l'emploi des moyens coercitifs', our emphasis.

23 Ibid., p. 127.

24 Esquiros, *Paris au XIXième siècle*, II, Paris 1847, p. 202.

25 Dr Baume, 'Compte rendu du livre du Pr Laborde, *Les hommes et les actes de l'insurrection de Paris devant la psychologie morbide*', *Annales médico-psychologiques*, VII, Paris 1872, p. 297.

26 Maxime Du Camp, *Les convulsions de Paris*, I, Paris 1878, p. 470.

27 Ibid., II, pp. 86–90.

Chapter 2   Outcasts from the Family

1 Ferdinand Teinturier, *Les Femmes*, Paris 1860, p. 3.

2 Trélat, *La folie lucide*, pp. 202–3, our emphasis.

3 6Q1 3.

4 6Q1 4.

5 6Q1 3.

6 Ibid.

7 Eugène Suë, *Les Mystères de Paris*, first publ. 1842, Hallier, 1978, p. 215.

8 Vallès, *Tableaux*, p. 67.

9 Elisabeth Packard, *Épouse, mère et folle; plaidoyer pour moi-meme. Asile*

de Jacksonville, 1860, translated into French by Julie Pavesi, Paris 1980, pp. 181–3.

10 Ibid., p. 190.

11 Paragraph 10 of the Law relating to Good Works of the 15 February 1851 in the Legal Code of the State of Illinois.

12 Elisabeth Packard, *Modern Persecutions in Insane Asylums Unveiled*, pp. 53–4, quoted by Thomas Szasz in *L'âge de la folie, l'histoire de l'hospitalisation involontaire psychiatrique à travers un choix de textes*, Paris 1978.

13 Packard, *Épouse, mère et folle*, p. 170.

14 Ibid., p. 176.

15 Ibid., p. 171.

16 Ibid., p. 172.

17 Ibid., p. 173.

18 Ibid., pp. 73–5.

19 Ibid., p. 20.

20 Rouy, *Mémoires*, p. 471.

Chapter 3   The Identikit Picture of the Madwoman

1 Panckoucke (ed.), *Dictionnaire abrégé des sciences médicales*, under 'Femme', Paris 1821–6, p. 267.

2 Yvonne Verdier, *Façons de dire, façons de faire; la laveuse, la couturière, la repasseuse, la cuisinière*, Paris 1979, p. 42.

3 Littré and Robin (eds), *Dictionnaire de médecine, de chirurgie, de pharmacie, des sciences accessoires et de l'art vétérinaire*, under 'Méno-pause', Paris 1865, p. 925.

4 Panckoucke (ed.), *Dictionnaire abrégé*, under 'Femme', p. 259.

5 Ibid.

6 Vallès, *Tableaux*, p. 65.

7 6R3.

8 6Q2 11.

9 6Q2 7.

10 *Grand dictionnaire universel du XIXième* (Larousse), III under 'Célibat', Paris 1866–76, p. 676.

11 J.-J. Virey, *De la femme sous ses rapports physiologique, moral et littéraire*, Paris n.d., p. 85.

12 Panckoucke (ed.), *Dictionnaire abrégé*, under 'Femme', p. 261.

13 Trélat. *La folie lucide*, pp. 43–4.

14 Etienne Esquirol in Panckoucke (ed.), *Dictionnaire abrégé*, under 'Folie', p. 91.

15 François Leuret, *Du traitement moral de la folie*, Paris 1840, p. 407.

16 Auguste Comte, Letter to Audiffrent, 6 May 1851, quoted by M. Albistur and D Armogathe, *Histoire du féminisme français du Moyen Age jusqu'à nos jours*, Paris 1977, p. 294.

17 Stéphane Michaud, 'Science, droit et religion: trois contes sur la nature', *Romantisme* (journal of the 19th century), 13–14, Paris 1976, p. 35.

18 6Q14.

19 6Q24.

20 Gustave Flaubert, *Trois contes: Un coeur simple*, Paris, 1965 edn, pp. 25–83.

21 Emile Zola, *La Conquête de Plassans* in *Les Rougon-Macquart, Histoire naturelle et sociale d'une famille sous le second Empire*, Paris, 1966 edn, p. 352.

22 'A propos de Gavarni: une mère folle', *Magasin pittoresque*, Paris 1847, pp. 291–2.

23 Ibid., p. 291.

24 Ibid., p. 292.

25 Ibid.

26 J.-L. Dulaure, *Histoire physique, civile et morale de Paris*, VI, Paris 1824, p. 393.

27 'Les industriels', quoted by Paul Sébillot in *Légende et curiosité des métiers*, 1895, p. 26.

28 *Magasin pittoresque*, Paris 1846, p. 241.

29 6R 74.

30 Ibid.

31 Geneviève Bollème, *La bibliothèque bleue, la littérature populaire du XVIième au XIXième siècle*, Paris 1971, p. 168.

32 L.-R. Szafowski, *Recherches sur les hallucinations d'un point de vue psychologique de l'histoire de la médecine légale*, Paris 1849, p. 154.

33 Vallès, *Tableaux*, p. 61.

34 T. Sydenham, quoted in Dechambre (ed.), *Dictionnaire encyclopaedique*, 'Hystérie', p. 241.

35 Etienne Lasègue, in ibid., p. 240.

36 Trélat, *La folie lucide*, p. 160.

37 6Q2 2.

Chapter 4   Life in the Asylum

1 Rouy, *Mémoires*, p. 51.

2 Ibid., p. 57.

3 F15 3901–2.

4 Vallès, *Tableaux*, p. 59.

5 Massot, 'Contribution à l'étude des maladies psychologiques dans l'Aine', quoted by Aimé Craplet in *Panorama de l'asile*, dissertation in psychiatry, Pierre et Marie Curie University, Paris, 1980, p. 51.

6 F15 3899, Report on the inspection of 14 April 1843.

7 Michel Caire, *Contribution à l'histoire de l'hôpital Sainte-Anne des origines au début du XXème siecle*, medical dissertation, Paris-Cochin, 1981, p. 65.

8 Rouy, *Mémoires*, p. 58.
9 Dr Renaudin, *Rapport sur les aliénés de l'asile de Fains* (Meuse), review by Girard in *Annales médico-psychologiques*, VIII, Paris 1846, p. 143.
10 A. Foville, *Nouveau dictionnaire de la médecine et de la chirurgie*, p. 216, quoted in G. Lamarche-Vadel and G. Preli in *L'Asile*, Recherches, no. 31, Paris 1978, pp. 92–3.
11 P. Pinel, *Traitement médico-philosophique sur l'aliénation mentale*, year IX, Paris, p. 184.
12 Ulysse Trélat, 'De l'envoi de 400 aliénés de la Salpêtrière et de Bicêtre dans les asiles de Saint-Venant et de Maréville', *Annales médico-psychologiques*, IV, Paris 1844, p. 380.
13 Pierre Berthier, *Excursions scientifiques à travers les asiles d'aliénés*. Paris 1862–4, p. 42.
14 F15 3899.
15 Ibid.
16 J.-H. Girard de Cailleux, *Rapport sur les aliénés traités dans les asiles de Bicêtre et de la Salpêtrière*, Paris 1863, p. 187.
17 F15 3899.
18 J. Manier, *Les bastilles modernes, mystères d'aliénés*, Paris 1866, p. 8.
19 Rouy, *Mémoires*, p. 178.
20 Berthier, *Excursions scientifiques*, p. 25.
21 Rouy, *Mémoires*, p. 18.
22 F15 3899.
23 *Compte rendu administratif et moral*, AD Gironde, IN 443, p. 9.
24 Rouy, *Mémoires*, p. 190.
25 F15 3900.
26 Claude Quetel, *Le Bon-Sauveur de Caen*, thesis, Sorbonne, Paris 1976, p. 377.
27 Rouy, *Mémoires*, pp. 231–2.
28 *Statistique des asiles d'aliénés pour les années 1854–1860*, Paris 1861.
29 F15 3916.
30 Dr Parchappe, *Des principes à suivre pour la fondation et la construction des asiles d'aliénés*, Paris 1851, p. 182.
31 F15 3900.
32 'L'assistance publique pour les aliénés de la Seine', *Annales médico-psychologiques*, VI, Paris 1854, p. 313.
33 Trélat, *La folie lucide*, p. 383.
34 Women's asylums are no different here, so we do not need to go into greater detail. On this subject, see Robert Castel, *L'ordre psychiatrique, l'âge d'or de l'aliénisme*, Paris 1976, p. 393, translated as *The Regulation of Madness*, Cambridge 1988. Also Lamarche-Vadel and Preli, *L'Asile*.
35 Du Camp, *Les convulsions de Paris*, pp. 481–2.
36 Dr E. Fredet, 'Un bal à la Salpêtrière', *Bulletin historique et scientifique de l'Auvergne*, 1889, p. 91.
37 Ibid., p. 93.

Chapter 5 Treatment in the Asylum

1 Rouy, *Mémoires*, p. 149.
2 F15 3899.
3 E. Georget, *De la folie, considérations sur cette maladie*, first published 1820, Paris 1971, p. 77.
4 Girard de Cailleux, *Rapport*, p. 41.
5 Trélat, *La folie lucide*, p. 37.
6 M. Macario, *Du traitement moral de la folie*, Paris 1843, pp. 19–20.
7 Trélat, *La folie lucide*, pp. 6–7.
8 Rouy, *Mémoires*, p. 583.
9 P. Moreau de Tours, quoted by Bernard Fréminville in *La raison du plus fort*, Paris 1977, p. 86.
10 Rouy, *Mémoires*, p. 183.
11 Ibid., p. 244.
12 Constans, Lunier, Dumesnil, *Rapport general*, p. 211.
13 Panckoucke (ed.), *Dictionnaire abrégé*, under 'Femme', pp. 265–6.
14 Trélat, *La folie lucide*, pp. 183–5.
15 M. Brière de Boismont, 'Recherches sur la folie puerpérale précédées d'un aperçu sur les rapports de la menstruation et de l'aliénation mentale', *Annales médico-psychologiques*, III, Paris 1851, p. 582.
16 G. Baillarger, 'Illusions et hallucinations chez une jeune fille chlorotique', *Annales medico-psychologiques*, V, 1845, p. 147.
17 Trélat, *La folie lucide*, p. 48.
18 See H. Ellinger's work, 'Onanisme: son influence sur le développement de la folie', *Annales médico-psychologiques*, Paris 1846, p. 126.
19 Ibid.
20 P. Briquet, *Traité clinique et thérapeutique de l'hystérie*, Paris 1859, p. 101.
21 Ibid., p. 150.
22 Ibid., p. 101.
23 Ibid., p. 100.
24 Ibid., p. 101.
25 J. Falret, quoted by Théodore Zeldin in *Histoires des passions françaises, 1848–1945*, Paris 1977–9, p. 116. See Zeldin, *France 1848–1945*, vol. 1: *Ambition, Love and Politics*, vol. 2: *Intellect, Taste and Anxiety*, Oxford, 1977.
26 The hysteria epidemic which struck the village of Morzine in Savoy from 1857 to 1872 was the object of many discussions. See Jacqueline Carroy-Thirard, 'Possession, extase et hystérie au XIXième siècle', *Psychanalyse à l'Université*, V, Paris 1980, pp. 499–515; Georges Wajeman, *Le maître et l'hystérique*, Paris 1982, p. 286; Zeldin, *Histoires*.
27 Pinel, *Traitement*, p. 70.

Chapter 6   Contacts

1 Rouy, *Mémoires*, p. 157.
2 Ibid., pp. 236–7, our emphasis.
3 Pierre Berthier, *Erreurs et préjugés relatifs à la folie*, Bourg-en-Bresse 1863, p. 30.
4 Rouy, *Mémoires*, p. 222.
5 Dr Renaudin, *Annales médico-psychologiques*, Paris 1863, p. 250.
6 Trélat, *La folie lucide*, pp. 44–5.
7 Ibid., pp. 45–6.
8 F15 3901.
9 Rouy, *Mémoires*, p. 164.
10 Ibid., p. 152.
11 Dr Mitivié justified the retention of Hersilie on his wards and his refusal to have her transferred to Rambuteau in these terms.
12 Rouy, *Mémoires*, p. 217.
13 Ibid., p. 371.

Chapter 7   The Endless Asylum or the End of the Asylum?

1 U. Trélat, 'De l'envoi de 400 aliénés de la Salpêtrière et de Bicêtre dans les asiles de Saint-Venant . . . , *Annales médico-psychologiques*, IV, Paris 1844, p. 370.
2 *Patronage et asile des convalescentes de la Salpêtrière*, bulletin of 10 March 1843, Paris.
3 Quoted by B. Odier, *Les sociétiés de patronage d'aliénés guéris et convalescents au XIXième siecle*, dissertation Paris-VII, 1982, p. 37.
4 Ibid., p. 50.
5 Ibid., p: 49.

GLOSSARY

Amenorrhoea   The absence of menstruation.

Anorexia, psychological   A condition characterized by loss of appetite. It can lead to cachexia (thinning) and to amenorrhoea.

Atony   Lack of strength.

Clitorism   A term referring to the abuse of the genitalia which women sometimes perform when they have a large clitoris (Littré).

Cretinism   A congenital form of mental alienation or mental retardation.

Dementia, acute   Passing states of psychological weakness (Esquirol, 1814).

Dementia, senile   General and complete psychological weakness occurring in elderly patients.

Demonomania   Delirium involving demoniac possession, linked to a persecution complex (Esquirol, 1838).

Dipsomania   Immoderate reliance on large quantities of liquids.

Erotomania   Depression centred on some love object (Esquirol, 1838).

Hysteria   Concept covering various sexual, psychological and neurological disorders. It was said to be 'undefinable'.

Idiocy   Congenital form of alienation, lack of intelligence where the patient's mental age is less than three years.

Imbecility   Similar to idiocy but with a mental age of between three and seven years.

Kleptomania   Pathological tendency to theft (Lasègue).

Lucid madness   Term applied to subjects who are lucid, but whose character and behaviour makes them anti-social (Trélat, 1861). It corresponds to a variety of character disturbances and to paranoia. Alternatively *thinking madness*.

Lypemania   Term referring to depressive, melancholic states, including confusion, obsessional neuroses, catatony and chronic persecution complexes (Esquirol, 1838).

Mania   Continuous delirium, agitated but without fever.

Melancholia   Psychosis characterized by an intense form of depression (see *lypemania*).

Mental degeneration   A doctrine defended by Morel and Magnan. It accounts for the appearance of certain types of mental problems by invoking a hereditary predisposition.

Monomania   Psychological imbalance accompanied by emotional disturbances and permanent and exclusive obsessions, involving partial delirium (Esquirol).

Mystical delirium   Delirium which is religious in nature, accompanied by visual or auditory hallucinations.

Nymphomania   An affection characterized by an uncontrollable desire for relief in sexual acts (alternatively, 'uterine madness').

Onanism   Solitary pursuit of orgasm through means other than normal coitus.

Paranoia   Problems characterized by anger, pride or over-sensitivity.

Puerperal madness   Mental problems following pregnancy and childbirth.

Pyromania   (1) Morbid attraction to fire; (2) uncontrollable urge to light fires.

Restraint, no   English theory rejecting the use of various means of restriction.

Tribadism   Female homosexuality.

INDEX

Adalbert of Chamisso, 70
adultery, 63
Aix-en-Provence, nuns at, 144
alcohol, and madness, 78–9
alienists (psychiatrists), attitude to
women, 160–1; attitude towards
working class, 87–8; and Droin
affair, 19; and education, 127–9;
and female excess, 119–21; on
longevity of women, 158; and
political symptoms, 22–9; power
of, 3–4; and reaction to
menstruation, 130–1; view of,
144–5
ambition, and madness, 70
Annales médico-psychologiques
(Cailleux), 96, 117, 133, 154
anorexia, treatment of, 131–2
Antiquailles-Lyon, conditions at,
90
Archambauld, Dr, 122
asylums, birth of, 3; conditions at,
90–1, 92–3; escapes from,
138–9; food and problems in,
104–6; hierarchy of, 89–90,
92–3; increase of inmates in, 1;
laundry and bedding problems
in, 102–3; perceptions of, 84–5;
and relationship with prisons,
19–20; shortcomings of 4–5; as
social regulators, 29–30;
transfers between, 150–2; where
built, 85–6, 92–3
Aubanel, Dr, 91, 143

Auxerre, hydrotherapy at, 124; as
model asylum, 97–9
auxiliaries, recruitment of, 141;
role of, 140–1
Azouy, Dr, and Hersilie, 145

Baillarger, Dr, 17
Balzac, Honoré de, 2
balls, 111–13
Baume, Dr, 27
bedding, problems of, in asylums,
103
behaviour, gender-based
differences in, 14–15
Belhomme, Dr, 129
Bertier, Dr, 143
Bicêtre, 39
Blois, 151; work at, 109
books, reading of, allowed, 114,
126–7
Bouches-du-Rhône, inspector of,
117–18
Bovary, Madame, 62, 67
bovarysme, 62
Brière de Boismont, A., 129; on
menstruation, 131; and political
madness, 25
Briquet, Dr, 136; and theory of
hysteria, 134–5
brochures, on asylums, 89
Bureau Central, 10, 71

Cadillac Hospital, 102–3, 105
cells, of Paris, 10–11